KING

WOODEN

TOYS

D1133820

15 Projects That Stack, Tumble, Whistle & Climb

STUDIO TAC CREATIVE

FOX CHAPEL
PUBLISHING

© Fox Chapel Publishing Company, Inc., 903 Square Street, Mount Joy, PA 17552.

ISBN: 978-1-4971-0393-1

Library of Congress Control Number: 2023943910

Managing Editor: Gretchen Bacon
Acquisitions Editor: Kaylee J. Schofield
Editor: Joseph Borden
Designer: Freire Disseny + Comunicació
Proofreader: Kelly Umenhofer
Indexer: Jay Kreider

HANDMADE WOODEN TOYS
Copyright ©2014 STUDIO TAC CREATIVE CO., LTD.
All rights reserved.
Original Japanese edition published by STUDIO TAC CREATIVE CO., LTD.
Photographer:
This English language edition is published by arrangement with STUDIO TAC
CREATIVE CO., LTD.
English translation rights ©2023 by FOX CHAPEL PUBLISHING.
Photography Credits:
Yutaka Yasuda
Tatsuo Ii
Motokazu Hara
Makoto Kubodera
Daisuke Takagi

To learn more about the other great books from Fox Chapel Publishing, or to find a retailer near you, call toll-free 800-457-9112 or visit us at *www.FoxChapelPublishing.com*.

We are always looking for talented authors. To submit an idea, please send a brief inquiry to acquisitions@foxchapelpublishing.com.

Printed in China
First printing

contents

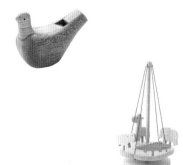

The Warmth of Nature Conveyed by Wood and Craftsmanship

Did you have a wooden toy that you were obsessed with when you were little? One that was simple yet captivating, engaging your senses? You could feel its texture in your hands—the weight, temperature, smoothness, and roughness. You could trace its subtle shape with your fingertips, feeling the straight lines, curves, acute and obtuse angles. You could hear and smell the natural materials it was made of. Everything about it was a part of nature, packed into a small toy by human hands.

Those who make things by hand feel a deep connection with nature, and that connection is passed on to the user, who feels the warmth that comes from it. Wooden toys are a perfect example of this—they are filled with this warmth.

Toys Are Fun for Children and Adults and Contain Powerful Appeal

Toys are meant to be played with. They possess a pure charm that compels us to hold and play with them. This purity is what makes them so captivating. They rotate, tilt, fall, roll, climb—and we listen to their sound and take in their cheerful colors. The accumulation of such simple pleasures calls to us.

The 15 toys introduced in this book may be simple, but they possess a magnetism that's hard to resist. They are cute, beautiful, cool, and unique in their sounds and movements. Even for adults, toys evoke a sense of wonderment and nostalgia.

Regardless of age, these toys have a magnetic quality that draws us close, beckoning us to pick them up and play with them over and over again. We hope you can experience this attraction with all your senses, too.

Introduction to Works

BIRD WHISTLE

▶ Instructions: page 42   ▶ Drawing/Pattern: page 156

▶ Instructions: page 42   ▶ Drawing/Pattern: page 156

This whistle toy features a gentle tone that exudes the warmth of wood and is designed in the shape of a cute bird. Crafted by layering boards together with glue, this toy is suitable for children aged between $1\frac{1}{2}$ to 3 years and can be enjoyed by kindergarten and elementary school students alike.

SHEDDING SNAKE

▶ Instructions: page 50
▶ Drawing/Pattern: pages 158–159

This cloth-skinned tree snake has a playful, humorous, and wobbly movement that's sure to make you smile. While watching it shed its skin might give you a bit of a shiver, its overall charm is irresistible and sure to bring a chuckle. Perfect for children ages 2-3, as well as kindergarten and elementary school students.

DOG PULL TOY

▶ Instructions: page 72
▶ Drawing/Pattern: page 153

A playful wooden dog toy that swings its body left and right as it's pulled by a string, adding a delightful twist to the classic pull-toy design. The smooth curves give it a gentle, whimsical appearance that's sure to capture the imaginations of children aged 1-2 years old.

SEESAW

▶ Instructions: page 78   ▶ Drawing/Pattern: pages 160–161

A group of lively animals are enjoying a seesaw ride together. Kerplunk!
Who's the heaviest of them all? This cute toy doubles as charming home
décor and is perfect for children from 1 year old to kindergarten age.

KATAKATA DOLL

▶ Instructions: page 59   ▶ Drawing/Pattern: page 164

This classic toy features a katakata doll falling rhythmically down
a pegboard with colorful balls, creating delightful sounds as it
falls. Recommended for children aged 1½ to 4 years old, it's a
timeless favorite.

CLIMBING TOY: UFO

▶ Instructions: page 62   ▶ Drawing/Pattern: page 154

Hang this climbing UFO toy on the wall and pull the strings
alternately to make it climb toward the stars. Clap once you reach
the top! Ideal for children in kindergarten and elementary school.

MERRY-GO-ROUND

▶ Instructions: page 66
▶ Drawing/Pattern: pages 162–163

This merry-go-round features charming animal figures. Simply twist and release to set it spinning! Designed for children from 6 months to 2 years old.

PUZZLE CUBE

▶ Instructions: page 46   ▶ Drawing/Pattern: pages 156–157

This intriguing puzzle cube offers endless possibilities for patterns and designs. Recommended for children ages 2½ to 3 as a building block and for children 3 and up as a challenging puzzle.

RAINBOW PUZZLE

▶ Instructions: page 90   ▶ Drawing/Pattern: page 152

Discover the fun of matching colors with this puzzle featuring seven beautiful discs in different colors. Each disc fits perfectly into a hole of the same color and size, providing a satisfying challenge. It's a toy that will keep you coming back for more. Recommended for children aged 1½ to 3 years old and above.

TRAIN

▶ Instructions: page 82   ▶ Drawing/Pattern: page 155

This delightful train set features multiple train cars that are connected by a sturdy leather strap. The charming design is sure to capture the imagination of children and adults alike. Recommended for children ages 3 and up, this train set is perfect for both playtime and display.

KITCHENETTE

▶ Instructions: page 96
▶ Drawing/Pattern: pages 175–177

This kitchenette will make any child feel like a real chef. The sink and stove knobs can be turned, allowing for realistic cooking and dishwashing play. With shelves underneath, there's plenty of space for storage and organization. Suitable for children ages 2 and up.

TOY HOUSE

▶ Instructions: page 130
▶ Drawing/Pattern: pages 165–167

This adorable toy box shaped like a house is perfect for storing your child's favorite toys. It's made with sturdy dowel joints to ensure durability, and the lid is secured with a handle that can be locked. Recommended for children over 3 years old.

ROBOT WALKER WAGON

▶ Instructions: page 122
▶ Drawing/Pattern: pages 170–174

A unique walker wagon toy with a lively robotic figure that moves its arms and legs when pushed. The design is captivating to both children and adults. Assembled with sturdy dowels, this toy also provides a great woodworking experience. Suitable for children ages 6 months to 2 years old.

SWIMMING FISH

▶ Instructions: page 112
▶ Drawing/Pattern: pages 167–169

A wooden fish toy that realistically swims in water when the handle on the large cog is turned. The gear and piston mechanism makes this a fascinating toy for gadget enthusiasts of all ages. Recommended for children aged 3 and above, as well as adults who appreciate intricate designs.

KUGELBAHN

▶ Instructions: page 104   ▶ Drawing/Pattern: pages 178–181

The Kugelbahn, a classic rolling ball toy that has stood the test of time. The ball is set in motion and rolls down the track, only to be carried back to the top by a clever mechanism. Its simple yet fascinating design captivates both children and adults alike. Suitable for children ages 4 and up, as well as adults who want to relive their childhood.

How to Use This Book

This book will teach you how to create 15 beautiful "toys" that utilize the natural texture of wood. Our collection ranges from simple and nostalgic toys to intricate, complex ones. If you're a beginner, start with a simpler project and work your way up. If you're an intermediate or advanced maker, challenge yourself with a larger project.

Each project page includes a list of materials, necessary tools, and detailed instructions. Use this information to prepare for your project. Additionally, the step-by-step instructions include tips, techniques for achieving a beautiful finish, and suggestions for making the process easier. We encourage you to choose the methods that work best for you and use them to create your own unique toys.

Note: metric conversions throughout this book are not exact conversions of US sizes. Instead, they are the closest common metric measurements.

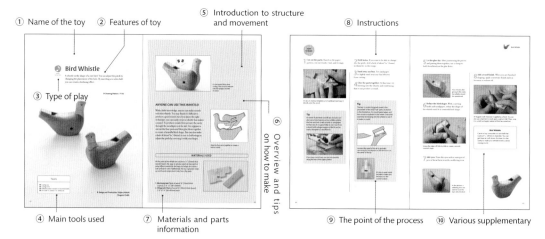

① Name of the toy ② Features of toy ⑤ Introduction to structure and movement ⑧ Instructions
③ Type of play
④ Main tools used ⑦ Materials and parts information ⑥ Overview and tips on how to make ⑨ The point of the process ⑩ Various supplementary

1 and 2: Explanation to convey what the toy is.
3: A classification how to play with each toy by toy type (see below). **4:** A list of tools needed, along with specified sizes and explanations of special. **5:** Explanation of the toy's structure and how it moves.

6: Overview and tips on how to make the toy.
7: List of materials needed. **8:** Instructions for building the toy.
9: Supplementary information such as tips, special points to note, finishing techniques, diagrams, etc.
10: Additional information

Icon Key

| Sound Comes Out | Put Away | Make a Shape | Repeat | Color Matching | Shape Matching | Balance | Move |

ABOUT THE TOY ADVISOR
Yumiko Adachi
Toy Consultant/Moikuiku Instructor

In 2011, Yumiko Adachi obtained a certification as a toy consultant, which qualifies her as a professional in the field of toys and play. This certification was obtained at the Tokyo Toy Museum located in Shinjuku Ward. As the first certified toy consultant in the Chichibu area, she gives lectures and advice on toys and play at public and commercial facilities in Chichibu-gun City and neighboring municipalities. She also runs a shop and hosts a play event called "Toy no Hiroba" four times a year. Additionally, she is part of the project team "Mokumoku Kikaku" which promotes wood education through the use of wooden toys made by craftsmen residing in Chichibu and using Chichibu wood.

Safety Note

The recommended age range for each toy mentioned in this book may vary depending on individual differences in interests and development, as well as the environment in which the toy is played. Please use it as a general guide only. Additionally, please exercise caution and ensure safety measures are in place when allowing young children to play with the toys.

Getting Started

7 Tools for Making Toys

These are the essential tools that are frequently used when making toys. Although other tools may be necessary depending on the project, having these tools should enable you to complete most basic works. Please refer to the Woodworking Tools & Techniques section (page 20) for detailed explanations of additional tools.

DOUBLE-EDGED SAW

A basic saw with saw blades on both sides, one for vertical cutting and one for horizontal. Use vertical cutting to cut along the woodgrain and horizontal cutting to cut against the woodgrain. When cutting wood, it is necessary to use these properly, lest you damage your sawblade or workpiece.

WOOD GLUE

This book aims to ensure the safety of children during playtime, so screws are used minimally in visible areas. Instead, we primarily use wood glue to assemble wooden pieces together. Additionally, a joint method called "doweling" is frequently used, which involves using a drill and wooden bar to join pieces. Please refer to the instructions on how to properly use this joint method.

COPING SAW

In toymaking, where wood is often cut along curved lines, coping saws are often used. It takes practice to make a smooth cut, but if you can master it, you can cut out almost any shape you want.

SANDPAPER

To achieve a beautiful finish, it's important to smooth out corners and surfaces with sandpaper. This book offers tips on efficient finishing using various tools, but sandpaper is still the essential tool for the job. Use sandpaper with a grit between 120 and 240 for best results.

RULER

Measuring and drawing lines accurately is crucial in making toys. To do this, you will need a ruler, preferably a straightedge that is at least 1" (30.5cm) long, and an L-shaped tool called a square. In addition, we introduce some tools at the end of the book that can help you draw lines more precisely and efficiently.

Attach a drill bit to the tip of the electric drill. They are sold as a set, but it is recommended that you buy them in small batches in the size you need.

CLAMP

A clamp is a tool used to hold wood firmly in place while assembling it. It is important to use clamps to create a strong bond. Once the adhesive is applied, do not shift the clamp until the adhesive cures.

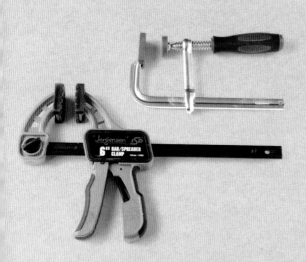

ELECTRIC DRILL

Making holes is an essential part of toymaking, and an electric drill is often the best tool for the job. While it is the only power tool among the seven essential tools introduced in this book, it is worth investing in. The drill bit, which comes in various shapes and sizes, is the part that does the actual drilling. We provide guidance on how to select the right drill bit and use the drill effectively at the end of the book.

Woodworking Tools & Techniques

Various woodworking techniques are employed in the creation of "wooden toys," providing an opportunity to engage with woodworking tools. Beginners are encouraged to embrace the challenge, while those with experience can further expand their skill set by actively incorporating new tools into their repertoire. The availability of a wider range of tools allows for greater precision in dimensions and angles, resulting in higher-quality finished products, increased efficiency, and enhanced enjoyment throughout the woodworking process. I encourage you to explore and experiment with different woodworking tools to discover the joys they can bring.

▶ **Courtesy: Yoshiteru Yamada**

TOOLS

- ■ **Measurement and Layout:** Ruler/Stopper/Caliper/Square/Measuring tape /Fastening ruler
- ■ **Adhesive:** Wood glue
- ■ **Clamping and Fixing:** Bar clamp/F-clamp/Vise
- ■ **Cutting:** Double-edged saw/Body saw/Dowel saw/Screw saw/Sujikebiki
- ■ **Drilling:** Electric drill driver/Drill bit/Drill stopper/Drill stand
- ■ **Shaping:** Woodworking file/Paper sander/Sandpaper holder/Electric sander /Router/Chisel/Plane/Bean plane
- ■ **Other tools:** Screwdriver/Craft knife

MEASURE AND DRAW

The precision of the measurements and line drawings before cutting the wood helps improve the quality of the work. Use these tools well and try to draw an accurate line according to the dimensions.

RULER

A ruler is an essential tool used for drawing straight lines and measuring lengths. There are different types of rulers available, such as straightedge rulers and curved rulers. It is recommended to have rulers of various sizes for different types of work, as it makes measuring and drawing surprisingly easier. When selecting a ruler, opt for one made of metal that can be used indoors. However, be cautious of extremely cheap ones that may have sharp corners or burrs, as they can scratch or cause injuries. As you gain experience, you may find yourself wanting to explore different types and sizes of rulers, as they offer a deeper level of functionality.

STOPPER

A stopper is a useful accessory that can be attached to a straightedge ruler. It serves as a stopper or guide when positioning the ruler on the material. By using a stopper, you can achieve precise measurements and maintain consistent dimensions throughout your work. It is especially valuable for tasks that require repetitive measurements of specific dimensions. One of its advantages is the ability to easily create right angles. When purchasing a stopper, ensure that it matches the type and size of your ruler, as not all rulers are designed to accommodate stoppers. Some rulers are sold with stoppers as part of a set, so it's worth checking the product details before making a purchase.

Slide the stopper along the straight ruler and attach it. Tighten the side screws to secure the position.

By placing a stopper on the edge of the material, like this, you can easily achieve right angles and precise measurements.

How to Easily Divide the Width Equally with a Ruler

1. Determine the desired number of equal parts you want to divide the width into, such as halves, thirds, quarters, or fifths.

2. Place the ruler diagonally across the width of the board. It is important to avoid tilting the ruler more than 45-degrees to ensure accurate measurements.

3. Find a numerical value on the ruler that can be easily divided into the desired number of equal parts. For example, if you want to divide the width into thirds, locate a value on the ruler that can be divided evenly by 3.

4. Mark the position on the board corresponding to the selected numerical value on the ruler. This will serve as a reference point for dividing the width.

5. Using the marked position as a guide, draw a parallel line across the width of the board. This line will divide the width into the desired number of equal parts.

By following these steps, you can easily divide the width of a wooden stick or board into equal parts, such as thirds, quarters, or fifths. Remember to use a ruler with clear numerical markings and ensure the ruler is positioned accurately to achieve precise divisions.

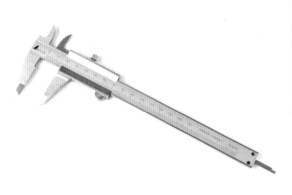

VERNIER CALIPER

A vernier caliper is a versatile tool that allows for accurate measurements of thickness, width, inner diameter of holes, gaps, steps, and depth. In woodworking, where precision is crucial, this tool proves useful in various situations. To use it, simply move the slider and read the scale while employing the appropriate "beak," "jaw," or "depth bar" based on the part's shape being measured. These three measuring instruments are the key components of vernier calipers. Additionally, the slider features a vernier scale, which enables measurements as precise as 0.05mm (depending on the specific product). This makes it an essential item for tool enthusiasts who appreciate measuring various objects with accuracy and precision.

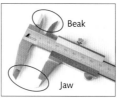

Beak

Jaw

Jaws are versatile for measuring both width and length, regardless of the shape of the material, by securely holding it between them. The beak is designed for measuring the inner diameter of a hole by aligning the line on the outside with the edges of the hole.

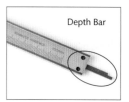

Depth Bar

The depth bar of a vernier caliper is used to measure the gap or depth between the tip of the caliper and the end of its body. This feature allows for measurements that cannot be easily obtained with a regular ruler. It is particularly useful for measuring the depth of holes, grooves or the height of steps, providing accurate and precise measurements in woodworking and other applications where depth measurements are important.

What is a vernier scale?

The vernier scale engraved on the slider of a vernier caliper allows for precise measurements up to approximately 0.05mm. To read the measurement, follow these steps:

1. Locate the "0" position on the vernier scale in relation to the main scale (the scale on the main unit). In this case, the "0" position aligns with the right side of the ½" (13mm) mark on the main scale, indicating a measurement of ½" (13mm).
2. Identify the position where the main scale and vernier scale graduations align with each other. Look for the overlap of graduations, ensuring there is only one overlap. In this example, the overlap occurs with the number 6 at the halfway position, indicating an additional 0.65mm.
3. Combine the measurement from the main scale ½" (13mm) with the additional measurement from the vernier scale (0.65mm), resulting in a final measurement of 13.65mm.

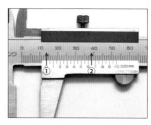

The depth bar measures the gap between the tip and the end of the body. It can measure things that cannot be measured with a ruler, such as the depth of holes and grooves, and the height of steps.

SQUARE

A square is a specialized tool used for measuring right angles. It consists of a thick base part and a part with a scale that allows for precise alignment and measurement of right angles. The base part is designed to provide stability and accuracy when positioning the square. Unlike an L-shaped ruler, the base part of a square is made of a thicker material. By ensuring that the square is placed exactly on the surface with the scale making contact, you can determine a right angle more accurately. When seeking an accurate right angle, it is recommended to use a square, as using a curved ruler may introduce errors if not applied correctly.

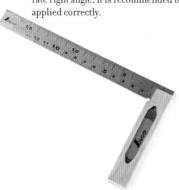

When using a square to mark or cut materials, it is important to firmly press the base part of the square against the material's surface. This ensures proper contact and minimizes any potential discrepancies or errors. By eliminating any gaps or movement between the square and the material, you can achieve more precise and accurate results in your woodworking projects.

SCRIBING SAW

A "scribing saw" is a tool that has a scribing blade attached to one end of a stick. By sliding the "ruler board" along the surface of the wood, you can create a line with a precise width. It is particularly useful for drawing center lines or other markings on thicker boards, providing more accuracy than using a regular ruler. The scribing saw is commonly used in woodworking projects, including the construction of the "Robot Walker Wagon" and "Shedding Snake" featured in this book. Its versatility and precision make it a valuable tool for achieving precise and clean lines in various woodworking tasks.

While referring to the scale, adjust the protrusion of the "rod" to the desired width. Once the desired width is achieved, it can be fixed in place by securely tightening a wedge or stopper. This ensures that the width remains consistent and allows for accurate and precise measurements during woodworking tasks.

Align the side of the ruler with the material and ensure close contact. While firmly holding down the scribe blade to prevent it from lifting, pull the ruler toward you in a controlled motion. This technique ensures a clean and accurate line as you scribe along the material.

TAPE MEASURE

A tape measure is a versatile tool for measuring long distances that may be challenging to measure with a traditional ruler. It features a flexible metal strip, often referred to as a "tape," housed in a rounded container known as a "case." The end of the tape is equipped with a hook or claws that can be extended or retracted. The hook is intentionally designed to have some play or movement to accommodate different measuring techniques. Whether using the hook to catch onto an edge or pressing the tape against a surface, the movement of the hook prevents the thickness from affecting the measurement accuracy. Tape measures are widely available, including affordable options found in various stores, making it a convenient tool to have in your collection.

COMBINATION SQUARE

A combination square is a versatile tool used for drawing precise 45-degree lines in woodworking. It combines the functionality of a fixed ruler and a square, allowing for accurate measurements and marking at right angles and 45-degrees. This tool is particularly useful when joining two pieces of wood at a 45-degree angle, as it helps ensure a proper and even splice.

GLUE

Using an adhesive specifically designed for woodworking is a reliable choice. These adhesives possess remarkable bonding strength that exceeds expectations, allowing for a strong and secure connection between wooden pieces. In fact, they often provide a stronger bond compared to using screws or nails. When using woodworking adhesive, you can confidently join wood together, knowing that it will hold firmly in place.

WOOD GLUE

Wood glue, also known as carpenter's glue, is a an opaque, water-based adhesive widely used in woodworking projects. It is relatively easy to use, but it's important to be careful as it can be slippery until it fully hardens. To ensure a strong bond, it is recommended to apply the glue evenly across the entire surface. Any excess glue that protrudes can be wiped off. It's advisable to apply an ample amount of glue for maximum adhesive strength. Since wood glue is water-based, it should be used and adjusted before it dries. In case of any excess or spills, it can be easily cleaned with a damp cloth. Some wood glues are also formulated to be water-resistant for added durability.

Water-resistant wood glue. Use this if your work will be exposed to water or moisture.

CLAMPS

A clamp is an essential tool in woodworking for securely fastening wood during drilling, cutting, gluing, and other woodworking operations. It holds the workpiece firmly in place, providing stability and ensuring accurate and safe work. Clamps come in various types and sizes, including bar clamps, F-clamps, and vise clamps. Having an extra clamp is always useful, as it allows for multiple points of secure fastening and increases the versatility of your woodworking projects.

CLAMP

A clamp is a tool used for securely fastening wood during woodworking projects. There are various types of clamps available, but for beginners, the all-purpose F-type clamp or bar clamp is recommended. These clamps have the same function and can be used to apply pressure and hold wood in place. When purchasing a clamp, it is important to consider the width of the opening, as it determines the maximum width that can be tightened. Additionally, clamps come in different sizes, so it's best to choose one that suits the specific woodworking task at hand.

F-TYPE CLAMP

The F-type clamp is a type of clamp that uses a screw mechanism on the handle to tighten and secure the clamp. The movable part of the clamp, which is marked with a circle, slides freely when it is loosened, allowing for easy adjustment and positioning. Once tightened, the F-type clamp provides a firm grip and holds the wood securely in place during woodworking tasks.

BAR CLAMP

The bar clamp is a type of clamp that features a sliding body that moves gradually as the lever is pulled, allowing for easy tightening of the clamp. To release the clamp and loosen it, simply press the release button located on the clamp (as shown above in the right photo). This convenient mechanism provides efficient and adjustable clamping for woodworking projects.

Clamp Variations

C-type Clamp

The C-type clamp features a simple structure with a C-shaped body and screws. While it has a narrower width that can be tightened compared to other clamp types, it is an affordable option. If you require multiple clamps for your woodworking projects, the C-type clamp is recommended due to its cost-effectiveness.

Clip Type

The clip type clamp is a simpler variation of a clamp. It utilizes a clip mechanism for tightening, and while the tightening force may not be as strong as other clamp types, it is still handy to have several on hand. The clip type clamp is convenient for lighter tasks and provides quick and easy clamping solutions.

VISE

A vise is a tool used to secure wood in place when cutting or drilling. It consists of two main parts: the vise itself, which is attached to the workbench, and the movable jaw that holds the wood. In this book, we will focus on using small vises suitable for the projects mentioned. Due to the intricate nature of the work involved in making wooden toys, a small tabletop vise can be used to provide stability to the wood during the process. By securely holding the wood with a vise, you can work more efficiently and with greater safety, as it allows you to use both hands while performing the tasks.

CUTTING

The primary tool for cutting wood is a saw, which comes in various types depending on the cutting method and the desired shape. It is crucial to select the appropriate saw for each specific task, as using the right tool in the right place can ensure clean cuts, minimize errors, and reduce the amount of finishing work required.

VARIOUS TYPES OF SAWS

Saws can be divided into two main types based on their cutting action: vertical pull and horizontal pull. The important thing to remember is that saw blades are typically large and come in different types for specific cutting needs. Vertical pull saws are designed for cutting along the woodgrain, utilizing a pulling motion towards you, while horizontal pull saws are used for cutting across the woodgrain with a horizontal pulling motion. Using the appropriate saw for the specific cutting direction is crucial to achieve clean and efficient cuts. Additionally, it's worth noting that saw blades cut wood in one direction as they move, making the cutting action most effective in one direction and less efficient in the opposite direction. Understanding these principles and using the right saws will allow you to handle various woodworking tasks with precision and efficiency.

Double-edged saw

A basic saw with vertical and horizontal blades on each side.

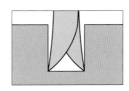

Body saw

The body saw, with its blade attached to the back, offers enhanced stability and accuracy for cutting straight lines. Its horizontal blade orientation further contributes to its ability to make precise cuts. This makes the body saw well-suited for detailed craftsmanship and achieving accurate results in woodworking.

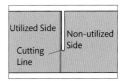

Dowel saw

The dowel saw is characterized by its flexible blade that bends without clamping. This design feature is specifically intended for cutting dowels.

Consider the Thickness of the Saw Blade

When using a saw to cut wood, it's important to consider the thickness of the saw blade. While a saw is often referred to as "cutting" wood, it actually shaves off a thin width of the material. To prevent the saw blade from getting stuck and making it difficult to move, clamps are added. However, it's essential to be cautious about the spread of the clamps, as they can result in further loss of material during the cutting process.

The presence of clamps creates a wider gap than the thickness of the saw blade, reducing friction and allowing for smoother cutting.

Utilized Side | Non-utilized Side

Cutting Line

To avoid cutting into the desired dimensions, it is necessary to shift the saw blade to the side that will not be used.

Handling Saws

When handling a saw, grip it near the blade, towards the back of the handle. Holding it this way helps prevent excessive swaying or deviation, resulting in wide or curved cuts. Avoid exerting too much force, as the blade should not dig deeply into the wood. To stabilize the blade and ensure precision, position your left thumb on the side of the cut and make controlled, fine movements during the initial cutting process. By following these guidelines, you can achieve more accurate and controlled cuts with the saw.

Pull the saw straight back to prevent bending the cut end, and initially cut slowly while checking the cutting line for accuracy.

COPING SAW

The coping saw is a saw with a thin blade that can cut curves effectively. Its prominent feature is its suitability for making curved cuts, making it a valuable tool in toy production where such cuts are common. Achieving smooth cuts with a coping saw requires practice and technique, so it is advisable to practice on scraps before working on actual projects. In most cases, the blade of a coping saw is detachable, allowing you to choose the thickness and select between woodworking and ironworking blades. Thinner blades are suitable for fine woodworking, but they may be more delicate and require careful handling to avoid breakage.

A coping saw features a very fine blade, similar to a jigsaw. Like a regular saw, the blade has a specific orientation or direction it should face during use.

Coping saws are primarily used for cutting boards. To ensure stability, secure the wood to a workbench using a clamp, preventing it from moving during the cutting process. Attach the coping saw blade in a downward orientation and apply downward force while cutting (if the blade faces upward, the material may lift and result in blurred cuts).

SCROLL SAW

The scroll saw is a stationary electric saw that offers superior performance compared to handheld jigsaws. It is highly recommended for woodworking enthusiasts, including beginners. The scroll saw is particularly valuable in toymaking due to its ability to effortlessly cut and shape curved lines. With its versatility and frequent usage, it is a valuable tool that can significantly enhance your woodworking projects.

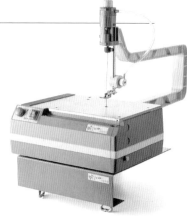

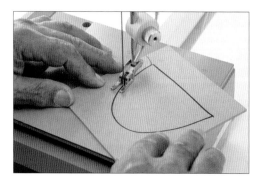

Since the material can be moved by holding it with both hands, even curved lines can be cut smoothly.

The speed of the blade can be adjusted, so you can work quickly on straight lines and slowly and carefully on curves.

DRILLING

As with cutting, drilling is frequently used in wood processing. Most of the works in this book use this technique, so you need some kind of drilling tool.

ELECTRIC DRILL DRIVER

The electric drill driver has become an essential tool for DIY enthusiasts due to its versatility. Along with drilling, it offers various attachments such as screwdrivers and drill bits, making it a versatile ally for craft enthusiasts, including woodworking. It's not limited to assembling furniture or interior repairs; owning one can be advantageous for a wide range of projects. While impact drivers are available for larger-scale tasks with rotational force and impact, for toymaking or screw tightening, opting for a drill driver is recommended.

How to Choose an Electric Drill Driver

When selecting an electric drill driver, there are a few key factors to consider. First, check the power of the drill. For drilling holes in wood, a minimum of 10.8V (volts) or higher is recommended to ensure sufficient power. This is important as inadequate power can make tasks like tightening long screws challenging.

Next, consider the type of battery: rechargeable or corded. If you use the drill driver several times a month, a battery-powered option may be suitable. However, if you find it inconvenient to deal with battery recharging or running out of charge frequently, a corded drill driver may be a more practical choice. Weight is another consideration, and if you can work within the reach of a cord, the corded option provides a reliable power source.

DRILL BIT

A drill bit is an attachment used with an electric drill driver. There are two main types of drill bits: "for wood" and "for iron," but both can be used for woodwork. Woodworking drill bits generally create cleaner holes, while ironworking drill bits come in a wider range of sizes, allowing you to choose according to the desired hole size.

For woodworking

For ironwork

Drill bits typically have a maximum size of 2" (50mm). However, for the 2⅜" (60mm) holes required for some projects in this book, you will need to use a "Forstner bit" specifically designed for that size. Forstner bits are suitable for drilling larger diameter holes beyond the range of regular drill bits.

DRILL STOPPER

A drill stopper is an attachment that can be fixed onto a drill bit to control the depth of the hole being drilled. By fixing the stopper at a specific distance from the tip of the drill bit, it automatically stops the drill bit from advancing further once it reaches the desired depth.

To use a drill stopper, simply secure it in place at the desired depth position using a screw. When drilling, the stopper will make contact with the surface of the wood, causing the drill bit to stop its advancement, ensuring consistent and accurate hole depths.

DRILL STAND

A drill stand is a tool used to securely hold and fix an electric drill driver. It allows you to lower the drill and drill holes with more stability compared to drilling by hand, which can result in fluctuating angles. If your budget permits, having a drill stand is beneficial. When purchasing, ensure that the drill driver is compatible with the stand. Additionally, there are stationary tools known as "drilling machines" that integrate an electric drill. These machines offer even higher precision when drilling holes. Some tabletop-sized drilling machines are available for less than 10,000 yen. Considering these options can provide you with a stationary drilling experience. Before purchasing, check the drill stand's stroke width to ensure it meets your drilling needs. By using a drill stand, you can enjoy the convenience of a stationary drill, resembling a drilling machine. Consider the drill stand's ability, indicated by the width of stroke, to determine the maximum thickness of holes it can drill before making a purchase.

Fixing the drill in the stand allows for a stationary drill setup, resembling a "drilling machine," offering improved stability and precision.

Tips and Tricks for Using a Drill Driver

Using a drill driver effectively requires proper techniques and strategies. Here are some helpful tips and tricks to enhance your drilling experience. These tips include using a backing board to prevent burrs, aligning the drill tip accurately, maintaining a firm grip and support, gradually rotating the drill, recognizing changes in feel and sound, holding the drill driver firmly with both hands, using a mirror for vertical drilling, and securely fixing small or round objects. By following these suggestions, you can achieve better control, precision, and overall success with your drilling tasks.

Hold the drill driver firmly with both hands to minimize shaking caused by the rotational force. Keeping your body close together without leaning back will make it easier to control.

For handheld vertical drilling, using a mirror in front of you allows for visual checks from two directions without needing to move your body.

When drilling holes in small or round objects, ensure they are firmly fixed using a vise or a similar clamping device for stability.

Dowel Joint Procedure

The dowel joint procedure is often used in the toys showcased in this book. Here are the basic steps for a dowel joint using a a drill with a small Forstner bit or a regular drill bit. Ensure the diameter of the drill bit matches the size of the dowel for a proper fit.

Drill a hole approximately ½" (11–12mm) deep when using a regular drill bit) in one of the materials where the dowel will be inserted. Place the dowel marker in the hole to mark the dowel locations.

  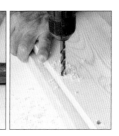

After marking all the dowel locations with dowel markers, align the other piece of material and gently tap it to transfer the marks. Drill corresponding holes using the marks as guides. If using a round dowel, pierce it with a drill bit. For dowels included in a set, use a dowel drill on this side as well.

Apply a small amount of wood glue to the corners of the dowel hole and insert the round dowel into the hole until it reaches the back (you'll hear a sound change).

Trim any excess protruding dowel using a saw specifically designed for flexible dowels without clamps. Finally, use sandpaper or a planer to smooth out the dowel joint for a finished result.

SHAPING

Achieving rounded corners and smooth surfaces is crucial for creating well-finished toys. Using the right tools is essential in ensuring efficiency, beauty, and safety for small children who will be playing with the toys.

WOOD FILE/ SANDPAPER

To shape the wood in the final stage, the use of wood files and sandpaper is essential. Wood files are ideal for rough shaping, while sandpaper is predominantly used. When using sandpaper, it is important to consider the type of surface you are working on. For flat surfaces and straight lines, use sandpaper on a flat wooden block, while for curved surfaces, wrap the sandpaper around a piece of wood with a similar curve. This helps ensure even application of force and more consistent results.

Sandpaper is available in different "counts," with higher numbers indicating finer grains and lower numbers indicating coarser grains. Starting with a lower count and gradually progressing to a higher count allows for a smoother finish. For example, beginning with #80, then moving to #120, and finishing with #240 will yield a significantly smoother surface.

An alternative to sandpaper is a "cloth file" that serves the same purpose. Although slightly more expensive, cloth files are durable and long-lasting. However, they are less flexible than sandpaper and may not be as suitable for fine curves.

How to Cut Sandpaper

To prevent damage to the blades, avoid cutting sandpaper with scissors or cutters. Instead, make a crease and tear along the fold using a ruler as a guide.

Place a ruler along the crease and tear. Once you get used to it, you can cut cleanly and straight.

SANDPAPER HOLDER

A sandpaper holder is a handy tool that facilitates sanding. With clips on both ends, it allows for easy attachment of sandpaper in a flat state. This simple tool proves useful for smoothing flat surfaces and chamfering long corners, providing efficient sanding capabilities. Additionally, it offers the convenience of easily attaching appropriately sized sandpaper on the backside for prolonged sanding tasks.

Attach a piece of sandpaper, cut to the appropriate size, to the backside of the wood file holder. This feature proves to be very convenient when undertaking sanding tasks over an extended period of time.

ELECTRIC SANDER

The electric sander is a highly efficient tool that greatly enhances filing processes. Resembling an iron, it is capable of fine work, including intricate details. Whether you're working on projects like the "Toy House" or "Robot Walker Wagon" featured in this book, the electric sander will undoubtedly provide significant assistance and improve your overall work efficiency.

Attach specialized adhesive-backed sandpaper to the backside of the electric sander. This allows for easy and secure placement of the sandpaper, ensuring efficient and effective sanding during use.

ROUTER

Blades or bits, which are replaceable attachments, are affixed to the tip of the tool. When the tool rotates at high speed, it effectively cuts grooves and corners, making it a powerful tool for rounding and chamfering work. The use of accessories such as guides and templates is crucial to mastering this tool's handling. However, with practice and the right techniques, it can achieve exceptionally beautiful wood-working results. This manual introduces the use of a file for finishing, so if you're interested, please explore the instructions provided in the following pages for basic handling and specific usage outlined within this manual.

Attaching blades (bits) of various shapes to the tip of the tool allows for wood to be processed into a consistent and uniform shape. The versatility of different blade shapes enables precise shaping and detailing in woodworking projects.

CHISEL

Chisels are highly effective tools for flattening wood cuts, making them particularly useful for tasks such as fitting missing pieces or creating intricate three-piece sets. They offer versatility and can be utilized in various ways. However, it's important to note that chisels, particularly Japanese craftsman tools, require specific handling and maintenance techniques, including the occasional sharpening. While they may present some technical challenges, chisels are recommended for those seeking to explore and master more advanced woodworking tools.

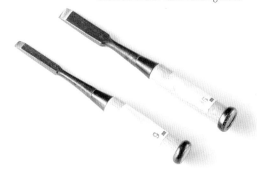

When using a chisel to dig grooves through hammering, utilize the slanted front side of the blade (left photo). For flattening a surface, employ the back side of the blade where it is flat (right photo). These different sides of the blade allow for specific cutting actions and surface treatments, ensuring optimal results in your woodworking projects.

USING A ROUTER

The router is a versatile tool that incorporates acces-sories like guides and templates. When combined with custom fixtures, it enables the creation of various shapes and allows for precise routing of not only straight lines but also intricate designs. The following pages provide essential knowledge and guidance on using the router's bits as featured in this book. We encourage you to explore and experiment with this tool to unleash its full potential in your woodworking projects.

Precautions for Handling

When handling a power tool, it is crucial to observe certain precautions. Always remember to turn off the power before plugging or unplugging the tool. Hold the base firmly to prevent it from lifting during use and maintain steady pressure against the wood. Avoid wearing work gloves as they can become entangled in the blade. Additionally, refer to the specific handling instructions provided for proper usage and ensure you carefully read and follow all instructions to ensure safety.

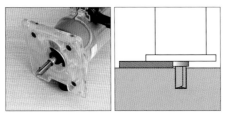

The blade of the router rotates clockwise, causing the outside to move counterclockwise and the inside to move clockwise. Moving the router in the opposite direction will result in poor wood cutting performance.

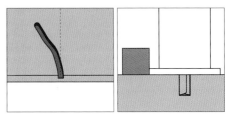

When using the router freehand, the rotation causes the blade to wobble to the left. To ensure a straight line, fix a rectangular piece of wood acting as a ruler on the left side.

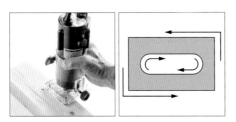

The guide enables the router to move along a self-made template. Refer to the instructions provided in the straight bit item on the right page for details on how to use it.

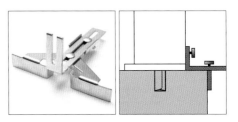

By attaching the "router guide" to the right side of the router, you can use the edge of the wood as a guide for carving parallel grooves or making precise cuts in wood.

STRAIGHT BIT

The straight bit is a versatile tool used for carving square grooves and performing edge cropping. It is particularly useful for creating window cutouts in the "train" or constructing the kitchenette. This bit is commonly employed for various groove-related tasks in woodworking.

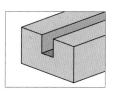

Carve square grooves using the straight bit. Adjust the depth by protruding the blade, while increasing the width can be achieved by cutting an additional groove right beside it.

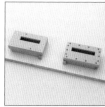

Utilize a router as seen in the project to the left. Attach a guide.

ROUND GROOVE (U-GROOVE) BIT

The round groove (U groove) bit is designed to carve grooves with a rounded bottom. The usage is similar to that of a straight bit. In this book, it is used to carve the lane of the "Kugelbahn" project. This versatile bit is well-suited for various woodworking tasks.

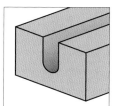

Round bottom version of the straight bit.

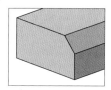

For chamfering tasks and other similar applications, there is also a "roller bit" available. This specialized bit is designed to create clean 45-degree corners, making it ideal for achieving precise chamfered edges. It provides a convenient and efficient solution for adding professional-looking beveled details to your woodworking projects.

ROUND FACE (BOSE FACE) BIT WITH ROLLER

The round face (bullnose face) bit with a roller is specifically designed for rounding corners, primarily used for chamfering purposes. It features a roller at the tip that acts as a guide, allowing for clean and precise shaping. The size of the bit should correspond to the desired corner radius (R) for optimal results. By firmly following the wood with the roller, you can effortlessly achieve beautifully shaped corners with ease.

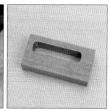

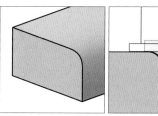

When working with the round face (bullnose face) bit with a roller, it's important to consider the corner radius (R) and select the appropriate sized bit accordingly. By using the roller's tip firmly along the wood, you can easily shape and create beautiful rounded corners. The combination of the correct bit size and the controlled movement of the roller allows for precise and aesthetically pleasing results.

PLANER

When it comes to smoothing wood surfaces and cutting edges, using a planer can be particularly helpful, especially for smaller projects like toys. This tool is recommended for tasks involving unique parts. It is versatile and can be used for flattening the cut ends of dowels and creating clean chamfers, resulting in a smoother finish compared to using a file. Ensuring the blade is sharpened and finely adjusting its protrusion are essential for achieving thin shavings that allow light to pass through while minimizing changes to the material's dimensions.

Adjusting the Blade

The adjustment of the blade in a planer is a delicate process that requires careful increments. Instead of forcefully hitting the blade with a hammer, even a light tap can bring about noticeable changes in its position. If you're unsure visually, you can try planing off some scraps to assess the results. The Mame Plane, in particular, offers the convenience of being easily fixed with a screw, making the adjustment process somewhat simpler.

The blade retracts when the wooden part (rise) next to it is struck, while striking the back of the blade causes it to extend.

To check the blade protrusion, observe the lower surface of the main body horizontally (bottom edge of the table). For this type of planer, adjust the blade by loosening the screw and moving it in and out directly.

Using the Planer

Since the planer is used by pulling, it is important to apply pressure on the front side of the wood. To ensure stability, attach a wooden piece of suitable size to the wooden base using screws or adhesive. Additionally, securely fasten the base to the workbench using a clamp. With a well-sharpened blade, minimal force is required for effective planing.

Firmly fix the base with the protrusion that holds down the material and position the workpiece. Hold down the front of the planer with one hand, and pull it straight forward while supporting it with the other hand, following the rise.

Aim for thin shavings during planing. If there are holes in the planer scraps, it indicates unevenness. The Mame Plane can easily smooth out unevenness by firmly pressing the material with your hand.

OTHER TOOLS

Here are a few more tools commonly used in toymaking. While these tools can be used by anyone, keeping these key concepts in mind while using them can help you achieve a better finish.

SCREW DRIVER

A driver is a tool used for turning screws. One important aspect to master is the size of the driver. Using the wrong size may cause the screw head to break. Precision screwdrivers, especially those used for small screws, come in various fine sizes, so it is crucial to use the appropriate one. When turning the screw, it should fit securely into the hole without movement. If you feel any resistance or slipping, it indicates an incorrect size. Additionally, the basic technique is to "push and turn" with the right amount of force. The ideal ratio for a smooth operation is often recommended as "7:3" (pushing to turning).

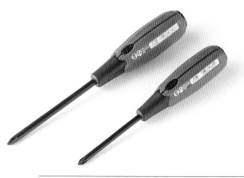

When examining screwdrivers of different sizes, you may notice slight variations in the roundness of the tip. It's important to choose the right size because using an incorrect size can result in improper engagement of the screw head. The tip of the screwdriver should fit securely into the screw head, allowing for effective turning and preventing slippage. Paying attention to these details will ensure a proper and secure connection when using a screwdriver.

CARVING KNIFE

The carving knife is a versatile tool in wood processing, requiring skill and dedication. Sharpening it regularly is important, as a well-sharpened knife can tackle various shapes and achieve precise cuts. It offers the freedom to create organic curves resembling hand-drawn figures, making it ideal for crafting toys like the "bird flute" and "swimming fish" featured in this book. Some cutting knives come with replaceable blades, providing convenience for continued use.

Insights from DIY Advisor Mr. Yoshiteru Yamada

In this article, we delved into the world of woodworking tools with guidance from DIY Advisor Mr. Yoshiteru Yamada. With a wealth of experience in DIY-related activities, including TV appearances, event participation, and workshops, Mr. Yamada shares his expertise and passion for woodworking and DIY. As the Representative Director of Dynacity Corporation and a qualified building engineer, he brings a multifaceted perspective to the field. Join us as we discover the tools and techniques essential for your woodworking projects.

DIY CITY: https://www.diyna.com/

Yoshiteru Yamada: https://diy-yamada.com/

Wood: The Basics

To get started with toymaking, let's explore some types of wood that are readily available. While there are various factors to consider when selecting materials, such as ease of processing, cost, and availability, we will introduce two recommended types of wood in addition to the commonly used woods featured in this book. If you're eager to start but unsure of what to purchase, this section is for you. If you're interested in a wider variety of tree species to choose from, please refer to page 38 for an introduction.

SPF

White, pale yellow. Mixture of spruce (S), pine (P) and fir (F). Easy to process and readily available.

Cedar

Light red to dark reddish brown. Easy to process and non-perishable. It has a unique, faint scent.

Beech

White or pale yellowish white with irregular brown markings. Easy to process.

Douglas fir

Contains hues of white, red, and yellow. It is easy to process and is recommended when you need to purchase large pieces of wood.

Douglas fir
(*Pinus densiflora*)

This species of Douglas fir is more commonly used for making furniture.

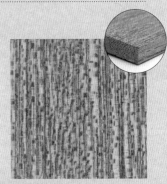

Lawang

They are called Meranti (Malaysia, Indonesia), Rawang (Philippines), and Seraya (mackerel) depending on the place of production. Uniform density and easy to process.

Material Size and Cut

The toy-making materials in this book are designed to be easily made from commercially available wood. To purchase lumber more efficiently, consider using lumber cutting services offered at home centers and mail-order stores. Simply provide the desired dimensions when purchasing to obtain the materials in the desired sizes. This will save time and potentially money, as you won't run the risk of cutting incorrect dimensions.

Additionally, a cheaper and readily available alternative to solid wood is two-by wood made from SPF (spruce-pine-fir). It is standardized, making its size consistent and easy to process. This makes it an ideal choice for beginners to get used to woodworking.

Main Size		
Labels	Reading	Thickness x Width (mm)
1 × 4	One by Four	25 x 102
1 × 6	One by Six	25 x 152
2 × 4	Two by Four	51 x 102
2 × 6	Two by Six	51 x 152

Main Size		
Labels	Reading	Length (mm)
1ft	1 foot	304.8
3ft	3 feet	914.4
6ft	6 feet	1828.8
10ft	10 feet	3048
12ft	12 feet	3657.6

* There may be a difference of about ±3mm

Finish with Oil and Wax

Applying oil or wax to finished solid wood can enhance its natural color and luster and protect the surface from wear and tear. This is especially important for toys, as they may be subjected to rough handling. The application of oil or wax also makes it easy to maintain the finish, keeping the wood looking great for years to come.

Walnut Oil

Walnut oil is a drying oil that is made from the seeds of the walnut fruit. It is often used as a natural finish for wooden toys, as it brings out the natural color and grain of the wood. You can buy walnut oil online or in your local hardware store.

Mineral/Tung Oil

Mineral oil and tung oil add a nice richness to the wood. Make sure to wipe the surface clean and dry before applying.

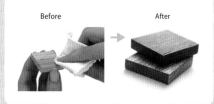

Before   After

Beeswax

Beeswax is an animal wax that is obtained from beehives. There are various beeswax products specifically designed for wood, as well as reasonably priced creams that can be used for finishing. Beeswax has highly protective properties that help preserve wood for years.

Wood Type

One of the great things about wood is that it's lightweight yet strong, and easy to work with using readily available tools. You can create beautiful, practical objects that are built to last. There are many types of wood available for purchase, each with its own unique appearance and processing properties. In this book, we focus on the best wood types for making toys. Choose the wood that best suits your preferences and intended use.

Solid Wood

Solid wood is a term used to describe wood that has been sawn from raw timber into a single board without any decorative pasting or cutting. It is a natural material with unique grain patterns and variations that add character to the finished product. Solid wood is durable and can be finished with oils, waxes, or varnishes to protect and enhance its natural beauty. Because it is a natural material, solid wood can expand and contract with changes in temperature and humidity, which can affect its stability over time.

Plywood

Plywood is created by bonding together multiple thin layers of wood veneer. The grain direction of each layer is arranged perpendicular to the previous layer, which gives it added strength and makes it resistant to cracking.

Laminated Wood

Laminated wood is made by gluing together thin strips of wood, creating a material that looks like solid wood. Like plywood, it has consistent dimensions and high strength, making it a reliable choice for woodworking projects.

Difference Between Conifers and Broadleaf Trees

Coniferous trees and broadleaf trees differ not only in their appearance, but also in their cellular composition, which influences their properties and characteristics. Coniferous tree species such as cedar and Douglas fir have different cell structures than broad-leaved tree species such as beech and lauan. Moreover, the annual ring pattern and tissue structure on the surface of wood, which is made up of cells, reflects how trees have adapted to their respective climates and environments over many years.

Conifer

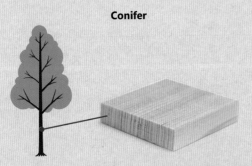

Since the cells that make up conifers are relatively uniform in structure, differences in woodgrain other than the annual rings are not very noticeable. This type of wood is generally referred to as softwood and is characterized by its ease of processing with a saw or knife.

Hardwood

Hardwood trees have a more complex structure than conifers, which gives their wood a unique grain pattern that varies depending on the species. Hardwood trees are generally referred to as "hardwood."

Tree Structure

Even with boards cut from the same tree species, the characteristics can vary depending on which part of the tree they were taken from and the internal material. Knowing the structure allows for enjoyable observation of the various characteristics of different materials.

1. **Heartwood:** The darker, inner part of the tree near the core. It contains inactive cells and is more resistant to decay than the sapwood. It is also known as "red meat."
2. **Sapwood:** The lighter, outer part of the tree. It has a higher moisture content than the heartwood because it still contains active cells.
3. **Quarter-sawn:** Lumber cut from passing through the center of the tree. This type of cut can only be obtained from large, old trees and is more expensive than other cuts.
4. **End grain:** The surface that becomes the cut end when the wood is cut at right angles to the grain.
5. **Rift-sawn:** Lumber cut parallel to the straight grain surface without passing through the center of the tree. The annual rings appear to be parabolic.

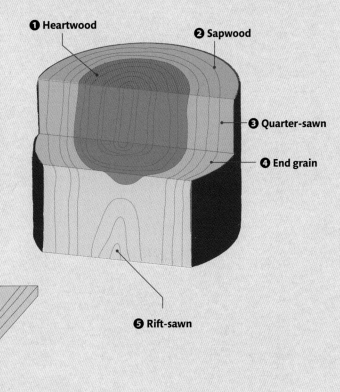

❶ Heartwood   ❷ Sapwood

❸ Quarter-sawn

❹ End grain

❺ Rift-sawn

Straight-grain Board   — End Grain —   Cross-grain Board

Drying and Deformation

Wood is prone to decay if it remains wet, so it is always dried. However, when the remaining moisture dries or the wood absorbs moisture, it can lead to cracking or bending due to expansion and contraction, also known as warping. These phenomena occur because the degree of shrinkage varies depending on the part of the wood. Cross-grain boards, in particular, are more prone to warping than straight-grain boards. To prevent warping during production, a warp stop can be attached to protect the work.

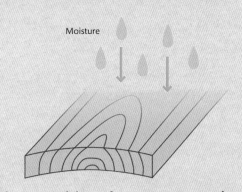

Moisture

Moisture-containing surfaces may warp convexly.

Toymaking and Wood

In Japan, people have adapted to the climate characterized by hot and humid summers and cold and dry winters. Surrounded by abundant forests, they have developed knowledge and expertise in selecting and utilizing wood species suitable for various purposes. The concept of "the right person in the right place" seems to stem from this understanding and has long been ingrained in Japanese culture.

Let's explore the relationship between wood and toys. Wood possesses properties that make it highly suitable for toy manufacturing, such as its insulating nature and pleasant tactile qualities. While human hands naturally produce moisture, wooden toys maintain a reasonable level of dryness. This is due to wood's ability to absorb and release moisture from the surrounding air. Unlike plastic and other materials, wood retains its unique composition, consisting of distinct cellular structures. This "breathing" characteristic of wood contributes to its gentle touch on the skin.

Furthermore, wood contains volatile aromatic compounds that give it a distinct scent. Unlike water, these scent components linger in wood for extended periods. From the process of crafting the toy to the act of playing with it, individuals can enjoy being surrounded by the delightful scent of wood. This quality adds to the appeal of wooden toys and enhances the overall experience.

Given these reasons, the selection of materials for toys often involves careful consideration. Now, let's introduce some wood species that showcase exceptional characteristics frequently sought after in toymaking. While it may be challenging to find these specific types of timber in physical stores, they can be readily purchased online. If you are interested in exploring these materials further, we encourage you to join us in discovering their unique qualities.

By combining the craftsmanship of toymaking with the inherent properties of wood, a truly enjoyable and sensory experience can be created.

Oil Finishes on Wood

Hinoki   Sapele   Teak   Cherry

Hard maple   Mizunara   Walnut   Wild cherry

Term Definition

Term	Definition
Boundary	Boundary between heartwood and sapwood.
Texture	Texture refers to the natural slight unevenness of the wood surface. It can be categorized into fine skin and coarse skin, representing smooth and refined or textured and rustic surfaces, respectively. Texture adds visual interest and tactile qualities to the wood.
Tiger Spots	Tiger spots are a pattern that emerges on the straight-grained surface of certain tree species with compound radial textures. The cross-sections of these patterns resemble the appearance of tiger hair, adding a unique visual element to the wood.
Ribbon Heather	Ribbon Heather is a phenomenon observed in tree species with cross-grain patterns. It is characterized by the appearance of alternating layers of cells that create striped patterns within the wood.

Tree Name: Walnut
Classification: Walnut Family
Distribution: Walnut trees are primarily found in eastern North America.
Color: The sapwood of Walnut trees is grayish white, while the heartwood ranges from dark brown to purplish brown.
Properties: Walnut wood often exhibits heather or striped patterns. Despite being heavy and hard, it is relatively easy to work with and has minimal deviation.
Usage: used for interior applications and gun stocks.

Tree Name: Sapele
Classification: Meliaceae
Distribution: Tropical rainforests of West and Central Africa
Color: Grayish white sapwood, purple-tinged reddish brown heartwood
Texture: Exhibits ribbon heather in the straight grain
Usage: Used for furniture and exterior materials for pianos, resembling mahogany in appearance.

Tree Name: Teak
Classification: Verbenaceae
Distribution: Indigenous to parts of the Indochinese peninsula
Color: Yellowish white sapwood, gold or dark brown heartwood with black stripes
Texture: Slightly rough with a smooth, wax-like feel and a distinct oil-like scent
Properties: Heavy and hard, known for excellent decay resistance, highly regarded as one of the finest materials.

Tree Name: Cherry
Classification: Rosaceae (Prunus genus)
Distribution: Mainly in the eastern part of North America
Color: Reddish light brown heartwood with clear boundaries
Properties: Heavy and hard with a fine texture, beautiful finish
Usage: Primarily used as a furniture material.

Tree Name: Quercus Crispula
Classification: Fagaceae (Quercus genus)
Distribution: Found throughout Japan
Color: Pale reddish white sapwood, brown heartwood
Texture: Coarse and heavy with tiger stripes on the straight grain surface
Usage: Commonly used in Western-style buildings due to its resemblance to American and European oak.

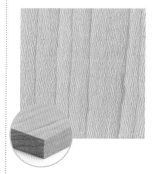

Tree Name: Hard Maple
Classification: Maple family
Distribution: Central North America, from northeast to southeast
Color: Heartwood tinged with reddish brown
Properties: Somewhat heavy with fine texture and beautiful heather
Usage: Commonly used for bowling approaches and pins, as well as musical instruments.

Tree Name: Japanese Cypress
Classification: Cupressaceae (Hinoki genus)
Distribution: Southern Tohoku and southern regions of Japan
Color: Pale yellowish brown to pale red heartwood
Properties: Easy to process, durable, warp-resistant, decay-resistant, beautiful luster, unique fragrance
Usage: Widely used in various applications, especially in shrines and temples, considered the best domestic conifer.

Tree Name: Yamazakura
Classification: Rosaceae (Prunus genus)
Distribution: Southern regions of the Tohoku region, Japan
Color: Pale yellow-brown sapwood, brown or dark brown striped heartwood
Properties: Slightly heavy and hard with a fine texture and clear boundaries
Usage: Mainly used for furniture and woodblocks due to its beautiful texture, often substituted with water sparrow.

Sound
Comes Out

Bird Whistle

A whistle in the shape of a cute bird. You can adjust the pitch by changing the placement of the hole. By inserting a wooden ball, you can create a birdsong effect.

▶ Drawing/Pattern: page 156

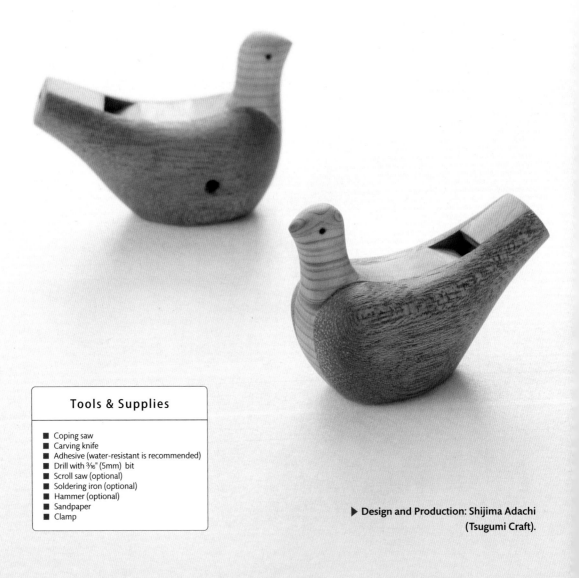

Tools & Supplies

- Coping saw
- Carving knife
- Adhesive (water-resistant is recommended)
- Drill with ³⁄₁₆" (5mm) bit
- Scroll saw (optional)
- Soldering iron (optional)
- Hammer (optional)
- Sandpaper
- Clamp

▶ Design and Production: Shijima Adachi
(Tsugumi Craft).

A cute sound like a dove cooing. The sound is imbued with the unique warmth of wood.

ANYONE CAN USE THIS WHISTLE!

You may think it's difficult to produce a good sound, but if you know the right technique, you can easily create a whistle that makes a sound. To produce sound, blow air into the cavity through the mouthpiece at the tail. Use a coping saw or scroll saw to cut out the four parts and then glue them together to create a beautiful bird shape. You can also make a hole of about ³⁄₁₆" (5mm) in one or both wings to adjust the pitch by covering it with your finger.

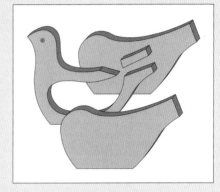

Glue the four parts together to create a hollow inside.

MATERIALS USED

All the parts of the whistle are cut from a ³⁄₈" (10mm) thick wooden board. Any easy-to-process wood can be used, but using different woods for the body and wings can create a cute contrast in color. Additionally, this toy is great for using up small wood scraps since it only has a few parts.

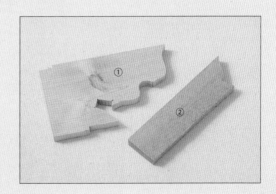

1. **Bird body/tail:** Plank of wood ³⁄₈" (10mm) thick (cyprus), 3 ⅛" x 2" (80 x 50mm)
2. **Wings (x2):** Plank of wood ³⁄₈" (10mm) thick (lauan), 2 ½" x 1 ¾" (65x 45mm) each

1 **Cut out the parts.** Based on the paper pattern, cut out 1 body, 1 tail, and 2 wings.

It's easy to make a template out of cardboard and copy it directly onto the wood.

Tip

It's easier if you have a scroll saw, but you can also use a handsaw to cut out a little outside the line and trim it with a knife or sandpaper. In that case, it is a good idea to cut it out from a board with a large margin so that it can be easily clamped to a workbench.

If you have a scroll saw, you can cut smoothly along the lines of the paper pattern.

2 **Drill holes.** If you want to be able to change the pitch, drill a hole of about $^3/_{16}$" (5mm) in diameter in the wings.

3 **Sand away any fuzz.** Use sandpaper to lightly sand away any fuzz left over from cutting.

4 **Glue the parts together.** At this time, try blowing into the whistle and confirming that it can produce a sound.

Tip

The key to producing good sound is the placement of the small tail parts. As shown in the illustration, the mouthpiece tapers and the corners are placed in the center. Check the assembly by blowing into the whistle to see if it makes a sound.

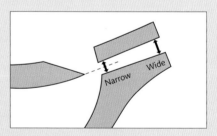

Increase the speed of the air by gradually narrowing the mouthpiece so that the horn is in the center of the tip.

Peek inside the hole to make sure the horn is in the correct location.

5 **Let the glue dry.** After positioning the pieces and pasting them together, use a clamp to hold them firmly as the glue dries.

After gluing the pieces together, the whistle should be operational.

6 **Refine the bird shape.** With a carving knife and sandpaper, refine the shape of the whistle until it is a smooth bird shape.

Scrape the edges off little by little to create a smooth, rounded shape.

7 **Add eyes.** Draw the eyes with a waterproof pen or burn them in with a soldering iron.

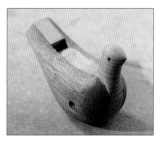

In this picture, a soldering iron was used to burn the eyes onto the bird.

8 **Add a wood finish.** When you are finished shaping, apply a nontoxic finish such as beeswax or walnut oil.

At Tsugumi Craft, beeswax is applied as a finish. You could also use walnut oil.

Bird Whistle

Carve or buy a wooden or cork ball that is about ⁵⁄₁₆" (8mm) in diameter. You can get these at craft stores. Enclose it in the cavity to make your whistle mimic a bird's cooing sound.

Puzzle Cube

Make a Shape

Color Matching

Shape Matching

A fascinating cube that can create infinite patterns. Let your child's imagination run wild and see what unexpected shapes they can create!

▶ Drawing/Pattern: pages 156–157

TOOLS & SUPPLIES

- Thin brush
- Acrylic paint (3 colors of your choice)
- Primer (such as gesso)
- Saw
- Scroll saw/coping saw
- Square
- Sandpaper

▶ **Design and Production: Shijima Adachi (Tsugumi Crafts)**

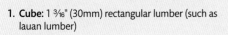
Snake design (left) and "LOVE" (right).

You can create a frame that fits the
cube perfectly and decorate the
finished design.

MAKE YOUR OWN BEAUTIFULLY
DECORATED FRAME.

This is a cube puzzle that can be completed by
painting two patterns using three colors of paint
on sixteen 1³⁄₁₆" (30mm) square cubes. The key
to this puzzle is the way the patterns are painted,
allowing for a wide variety of complicated patterns
to be expressed. Once completed, the design can be
displayed in a wooden frame, or the cubes can be
broken apart to start a new creation. Encouraging
your child's free and unrestrained creativity may
result in interesting shapes that adults could never
have imagined. Make sure to let the acrylic paint dry
completely before using.

Cube Puzzle

Sunrise	Snake	Flower	Crab	Thunder
Profile	Windmill	Kneeling	Bird	Girl
Car	House	Boy	Butterfly	Fish
0	1	2	3	4
Love	Kiss	ABCD	B	Moon

Variations that can be made by replacing
the colors of the same design

Materials Used

*The cubes are either cut from 1 ³⁄₁₆" (30mm) square lumber
or sold already in cube form. While it's possible to change the
size of the cubes, keep in mind that the wooden frame shown
in the instructions is designed for this cube size, so you would
need to adjust the size of the frame accordingly if you change
the cube size.*

1. **Cube:** 1 ³⁄₁₆" (30mm) rectangular lumber (such as
   lauan lumber)

1 **Draw a perpendicular line.** On your wood, draw a line 1³⁄₁₆" (30mm) from the edge that is perpendicular to the edge.

Tip

When drawing a right-angled cut line using a square, try to use the same corner as a reference as much as possible to reduce line errors. Additionally, it's important to draw lines on all four sides to ensure accuracy.

After drawing a line from one corner toward the front, draw a line from the same corner toward the back. By using the same angle as a reference, it reduces the possibility of an angle error. Repeat the same process for the opposite corner and draw lines on all four sides of the lumber to ensure accuracy.

Marking Correct Lines

In woodworking, when a line is misdrawn and ends up with a double line, a horizontal V with an open end pointing towards the correct side is used to indicate the correct line. In the photo below, the line on the left is incorrect and has a V drawn over it with its open end facing towards the right. The line on the right is correct.

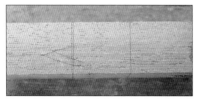

In this photo, the right line is correct.

2 **Cut out the cubes.** Cut along the lines you've made to create your cube. After it's cut out, make 15 more pieces the same way.

Tip

If you cut the cube all at once, the cut end will be skewed, so rotate the material and cut it little by little from all four sides.

3 **Apply primer.** Apply the undercoat of primer and allow it to dry. Once dried, remove any fuzzy areas by sanding lightly with sandpaper. This will ensure a clean and even finish.

This is a cube with a white primer undercoat. This will allow for the paint to be applied in smooth, clean coats.

4 **Color the cubes.** Color them by referring to the coloring diagram on page 156. Make 12 panels ① and 4 panels ②.

Tip

To make it easier to distinguish between colors, you can use color pattern paper to draw the boundary lines before applying the paint. Then, carefully review the development plan and color accordingly to avoid mistakes.

Apply a paper pattern to the cube and draw a boundary line. Pay close attention to the coloring instructions on the development drawing.

LET'S MAKE A WOODEN FRAME TO DECORATE THE CUBE!

To accommodate 16 cubes (4 x 4), the frame should be slightly larger than the size of the cubes. For $^{13}/_{16}$" (30mm) square cubes, a frame size of approximately 4 ³/₄" (122mm) square is appropriate. The upper and lower inner frames can also be decorated with wood to enhance the overall design. Let the cube protrude a little so it does not collapse,

You can use any shape for the inner frame as long as it meets the above requirements. Once you have the inner frame in place, retract the left and right sides slightly to allow for easy removal. Next, we will explain how to create a wooden frame with a border around the inner frame.

TOOLS

■ Drill with ¼" (6mm) bit

▶ Drawing/Pattern: page 157

Materials Used

The inner frame, border, and back board are typically made of 3/16" (5mm) thick panels. However, you can change the material or color to suit your preferences.

1. **Outer frame:** Rectangular lumber of about 1 ³/₁₆" (30mm) square
2. **Inner frame, border, back board:** ³/₁₆" (5mm) thick wood
3. **Stopper:** ³/₁₆" x ³/₁₆" (5 x 5mm) square material
4. **Dowel:** ¼" (6mm)
5. **Small nails or wood glue**

How to Make

1 **Cut out the pieces.** Cut out the outer frame, inner frame, border, back blank, and stopper to the dimensions shown in the figure.

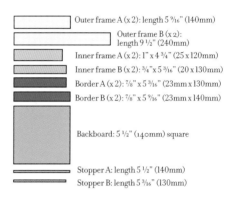

Outer frame A (x 2): length 5 ⁹/₁₆" (140mm)
Outer frame B (x 2): length 9 ½" (240mm)
Inner frame A (x 2): 1" x 4 ³/₄" (25 x 120mm)
Inner frame B (x 2): ³/₄" x 5 ³/₁₆" (20 x 130mm)
Border A (x 2): ⅞" x 5 ³/₁₆" (23mm x 130mm)
Border B (x 2): ⅞" x 5 ⁹/₁₆" (23mm x 140mm)

Backboard: 5 ½" (140mm) square

Stopper A: length 5 ½" (140mm)
Stopper B: length 5 ³/₁₆" (130mm)

2 **Combine outer frames A and B.** Combine outer frames A and B to create a frame that has an inner space of 5½" (140mm) squared, which is large enough to accommodate the backboard. Ensure that the top and bottom protrusions of the vertical outer frame B are ³/₄" (20mm) each.

Tip

Assemble with dowels or wood glue. How to hit the dowels is described on page 29.

3 **Affix the stopper.** Secure the stopper to the inside edge of the shell using nails or wood glue.

4 **Assemble the back board.** It should be 5½" (140mm) squared.

5 **Affix the border.** Place the border inside the outer frame, put the inner frame inside it, and fix it with nails or wood glue to complete.

Tip

If each part has the correct length, assemble the pieces according to the drawing on page 157. It is acceptable for there to be some gaps, as long as everything is securely fixed in place.

Make a
Shape

Move

Shedding Snake

Slithering and wiggling, this wooden snake toy is a silly and fun addition to any collection. You won't be able to resist its charm!

▶ Drawing/Pattern: pages 158–159

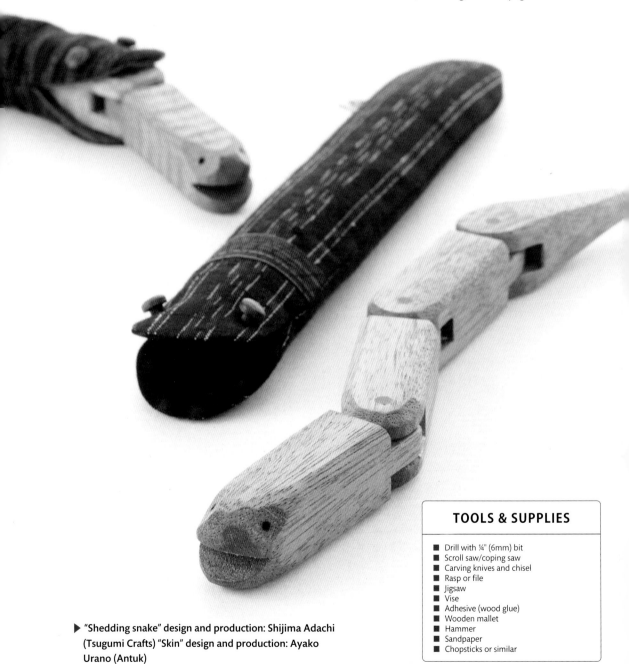

▶ "Shedding snake" design and production: Shijima Adachi (Tsugumi Crafts) "Skin" design and production: Ayako Urano (Antuk)

TOOLS & SUPPLIES

- Drill with ¼" (6mm) bit
- Scroll saw/coping saw
- Carving knives and chisel
- Rasp or file
- Jigsaw
- Vise
- Adhesive (wood glue)
- Wooden mallet
- Hammer
- Sandpaper
- Chopsticks or similar

SLITHER

SWOOSH!

This wooden snake twists and turns and can stretch out like a real one. The surface is covered in cloth, while the inside is made of wood.

Watch in amazement as the snake sheds its skin by popping out of its mouth. Both kids and adults will be fascinated by this creepy, yet cute toy.

THE THREE-PIECE JOINT AND HOW TO MAKE THE "SKIN"

This toy snake is made by connecting the head, body, and tail parts with joints using a three-piece jointing method. The joint part is made by inserting a dowel into the fulcrum, creating just the right amount of resistance for the snake to maintain its shape. A tool called a pull saw is useful when making the grooves and protrusions. To make the "skin" of the snake, a paper pattern will be provided. This involves sewing rather than woodworking, but it is still an enjoyable project. By ensuring the gap between the concave and convex parts is balanced, the snake will move smoothly and maintain its desired shape.

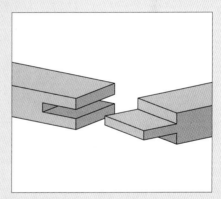

This toy utilizes a three-piece jointing technique to connect the concave and convex parts together. A fulcrum rod is inserted to form the joint and ensure that the snake can move and maintain its desired shape.

Materials Used

The snake is made by cutting the body parts from 1" (25mm) square lumber. Any material can be used except for extremely soft materials and hard materials that are difficult to work with. The fulcrum rod can be a dowel of about ¼" (6mm) in diameter or can be cut from ⁹/₃₂" (7mm) square lumber. Precision is not required as long as the joint can move smoothly.

1. **Head, body, tail:** 1" square (25mm square) lumber
2. **Joint fulcrum bar:** dowel of ¼" (6mm) wood

1 **Cut out the tail pieces.** Cut out three pieces of 3 ¹³/₁₆" (97mm) length and one piece of 3¾" (95mm) length from square lumber. These cuts are for the tail.

2 **Mark the grooves.** Draw lines for cutting grooves (protrusions) on one side of the head and tail and on both sides of the body.

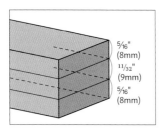

⁵/₁₆"
(8mm)

¹¹/₃₂"
(9mm)

⁵/₁₆"
(8mm)

Length on both concave and convex sides.

1" (25mm) from both ends

Draw a line at ⁵/₁₆" (8mm). Pull only on one side.

Tip

Rather than using a ruler, lines can be drawn more accurately by using a woodworking tool called a marking gauge that allows you to easily draw lines of even width. This is a very useful tool, so give it a try. See below for details on how to use a marking gauge.

Measure and mark only one place, ⁵/₁₆" (8mm) from the edge. Use a cutting knife, cutter, or mechanical pencil.

Align the sawing blade with the mark and draw parallel lines on all three sides of the wood.

Draw the line.

3 **Mark top and bottom surfaces.** To create the top and bottom surfaces, refer to Drawing B "Top and Bottom Stencil" (page 158) to transfer the hole positions and outlines. Note that the surface where the line is drawn will become the side of the snake, so the surface forming a right angle with it will be the top or bottom surface.

Pre-drill small holes at the positions marked on the template. Place the template on the top and bottom surfaces and trace the hole positions and round outline. Drill a ¼" (6mm) hole at the marked positions.

When drilling, drill from both sides or each half to a certain depth and connect them in the center until the bit penetrates.

4 **Cut along the lines you've drawn.** To cut along the line to a depth of 1" (25mm), secure the material vertically using a vise or clamps. Then, using a saw, carefully cut along the line while pulling the saw longitudinally. It is important to follow the line precisely and not to cut beyond the marked depth of 1" (25mm). Take your time and work slowly to ensure a clean and precise cut. Fix the material vertically and pull it longitudinally along the line. Cut with a saw to a depth of 1" (25mm).

Convex Side		Concave Side	
X	X	X	

When cutting, it's important to cut the concave side inside the line and the convex side outside the line. Cutting directly on the line may cause errors due to the thickness of the saw blade.

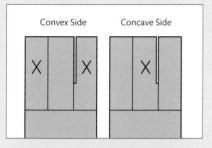

When cutting, it is important to firmly secure the material with a vise or other tools and to closely monitor the lines drawn on all three sides to ensure that the cut stays on track and doesn't shift or bend.

5 **Cut the convex and concave sides.** To cut the convex side, use a horizontal saw and cut from both sides. This will allow you to cut off the unnecessary parts easily. For the concave side, use a jigsaw or rough-cut it with a drill and then use a chisel to scrape it off. Make sure to cut slowly and carefully, and keep an eye on the lines drawn on the material to ensure the cut is accurate.

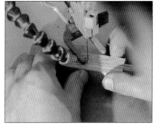

A scroll saw can be convenient for cutting off the deep part on the concave side. If a scroll saw is not available, you can drill a few holes in suitable places and then carefully scrape off the remaining material with a chisel.

A body piece that has been processed on both sides. The head is processed only on the convex side, and the tail is processed only on the concave side.

6 **Shape the joint.** Based on the lines of the top and bottom pattern paper, scrape off the excess wood around the joint part to make it a precise round shape.

With a carving knife, cut out a semicircle with a hole in the center.

7 **Cut the head.** Cut the head into a *V* shape, starting from the tip to make a mouth. Use a saw to make this cut. For the tail, cut diagonally on all four sides to make the tip thinner. Refer to Drawing A (page 158) for the desired shape.

8 Round the pieces. Use a knife or file to remove any sharp corners and to shape them to the desired form. Be careful not to remove too much material or damage the joint part. Check the shape regularly and adjust as necessary.

To add interest, you can use a circular chisel or carving knife to mark the entire surface and create a scale-like pattern.

9 Test fit the joint. After shaping the joint part, test the fit by attempting to insert it into the corresponding joint on the other piece. If it is too tight, you may need to trim it slightly more to adjust the fit. Additionally, when bending the snake at the joint with the hole as a fulcrum, make sure that it can turn smoothly around the corner without getting stuck or binding.

If a piece hits the corner of another piece, preventing it from bending, shave off the part that is causing the obstruction.

10 Cut the rod. A dowel or square bar of ¼" (6mm) should be cut to the appropriate size, inserted into the hole, and used to connect the joint.

Tip

To loosen a tight joint, gently tap it with a wooden mallet. Apply wood glue to one edge of the joint to prevent it from pulling out, and it will be less likely to come loose. Use sandpaper to flatten the end of the stick after you've cut off the protruding excess.

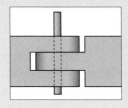

After inserting the rod, cut off the protruding bit.

11 Apply a finish. Finally, add a nontoxic finish such as beeswax or walnut oil. If desired, you can paint the pieces.

When beeswax is applied, it gives a moist luster and improves texture. You can also use walnut oil.

LET'S MAKE A SNAKE SKIN!

You can create a snake that sheds its skin by itself, but for further enjoyment, you can pull it out of its skin and play with it. To make the skin, please refer to Drawing C on page 159. Note that the cuff should not be sewn. For this, you will need basic sewing supplies (needle and thread) as well as the appropriate amount of your desired fabric.

HOW TO MAKE

1 **Cut out the fabric.** You will need two pieces for the top and two for the interior lining.

2 **Sew the pieces together.** Overlap the top piece with the lining piece, with the right sides facing each other. Sew them together in a *U* shape, leaving the mouth part unsewn and open. You should also leave a slit unsewn for turning, as demonstrated in the diagram.

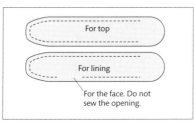

For top

For lining

For the face. Do not sew the opening.

3 **Sew the snake's head.** Take one of the top fabric pieces and one of the lining fabric pieces that make up the front of the snake's head. Sew them together along one side, then sew the other side together. Do not sew the cuff, and be sure to leave ample room so the snake will be able to fit.

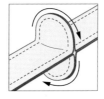

4 **Cut the tip of the mouth and tail.** Leave a kerf of ⅜" (10mm), and make ³⁄₁₆" (5mm) cuts at intervals. Your child can help by flipping the fabric over for you to cut the other side.

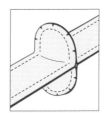

5 **Turn the fabric inside out.** Pull the inside through the turning opening so that the entire piece is right side out. Use chopsticks or a similar tool to shape the fabric, especially at the tip.

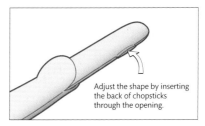

Adjust the shape by inserting the back of chopsticks through the opening.

6 **Sew the turning opening.** Sew the opening you left earlier for turning the fabric right side out. You can sew the opening closed either by hand or with a sewing machine using a stitch width of about ¹⁄₁₆" (2mm). Stitch and close the opening securely.

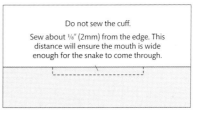

Do not sew the cuff.

Sew about ⅛" (2mm) from the edge. This distance will ensure the mouth is wide enough for the snake to come through.

7 **Sew the eyes.** Finish by sewing the buttons on for the eyes.

The trick is to make the area around the face as comical as possible.

Cube Puzzle (Tsugumi Crafts)

Shedding Snake (Tsugumi Crafts).

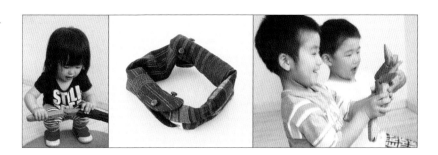

Bird Whistle (Tsugumi Crafts).

Katakata Doll

Sound
Comes Out

Balance

Move

Repeat

Watch as the dolls dance their way down the vibrant balls, creating a symphony of clattering and echoing wooden tones!

▶ Drawing/Pattern: page 164

TOOLS & SUPPLIES

- Saw
- Scroll saw/coping saw
- Drill with ⅟₁₆" (2mm) and ⁵⁄₁₆" (8mm) bit
- Adhesive
- Hammer
- Wooden mallet
- Sandpaper

▶ **Design and Production: Kenichi Iwai (Kiccoro)**

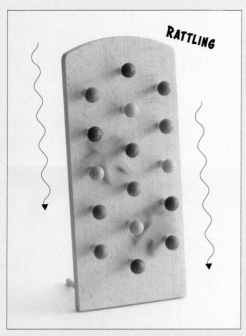

RATTLING

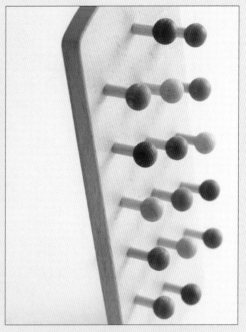

When dropped, the katakata doll emits a gentle rattling sound and descends slowly, as if holding onto an invisible stick.

In order to skillfully slip through the gaps, you must figure out the best place to drop the doll.

DOWELS AND BALL POSITIONS

The goal of this toy is to position the wooden doll correctly to make it tumble down the pegboard smoothly. Start by practicing hitting the dowel that connects the board and the wooden ball. The main feature of this project is the backboard, which you will need to drill holes into so you can insert the dowels. To make it, follow the instructions for attaching the stick and ball. It's important to learn how to properly position the dowels on the board. You can also add more columns to the pegboard if you like.

Materials Used

Here, the wood is European beech. We've listed the materials required to make two dolls, but you can make as many as you'd like. It is perfectly fine to change the wooden balls to cubes, if you desire, as this part will not change the doll's movement as it falls.

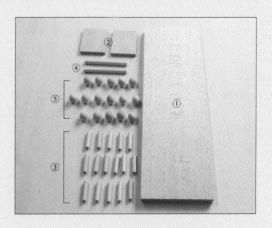

1. **Backboard:** a material that's 12 ½" x 5 ½" (320 x 140mm) and ⁹⁄₁₆" (15mm) thick.
2. **Doll:** a material of 2 ⅜" x 2 ⅜" (60 x 60mm), with a thickness of ⁹⁄₃₂" (7mm). You will need two pieces to make two dolls, and you can add as many dolls as you like.
3. **Round bars:** ⁵⁄₁₆" (8mm) dowels that are 1 ³⁄₁₆" (30mm) long; you will need 16 of these.
4. **Round bars:** a ⁵⁄₁₆" (8mm) dowel that is 3 ⁹⁄₁₆" (90mm) long, you will need two of these.
5. **Wooden ball:** about ¹¹⁄₁₆" (18mm) in diameter, you will need 16 of these.

Preparing the backboard

1 Cut out the backboard. Cut out the backboard as illustrated in the drawing on page 164.

2 Drill the backboard holes. Using the drawing as a guide, drill ³⁄₈" (10mm) holes into the backboard. Start by drawing three vertical lines on the backboard, and position the wooden ball at the bottom of the center line. Keeping to the guide will make the process easier.

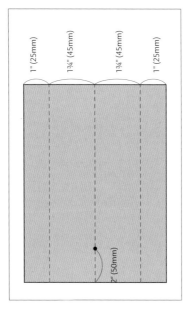

Mark the spots to drill on the guidelines as shown.

3 Determine the drilling depth. Use the second mark that you drew on the backboard as a guide to determine the drilling depth.

Tip

When drilling holes with a handheld drill, you can make a guide out of scrap material to ensure that the hole is drilled to the correct depth. It's important that you don't drill all the way through the material.

Guides are recommended for blind drilling.

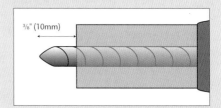

Cut and drill the wood so the drill bit is exposed for the depth of the hole.

4 Drill into the back of the board. On the back side of the backboard, measure and mark a distance of ⁹⁄₁₆" (15mm) from both the left and right bottom corners, and drill a ³⁄₈" (10mm) deep hole using a ⁵⁄₁₆" (8mm) drill bit.

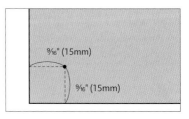

Location for drilling. Insert a dowel into this hole to make a stand.

Make a Doll

5 **Cut out the doll.** Cut out a doll based on the doll pattern paper. If desired, make 1/16" (2mm) holes for the eyes.

6 **Chamfer the edges.** Chamfer the edges of the dolls and board. Then, sand the surfaces smooth.

For added fun, change the arms to other designs. Just be sure to keep the same measurements.

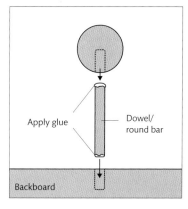

Insert the dowel so that it connects the holes drilled in the backboard and the wooden ball.

10 **Attach the stand.** Complete the project by inserting the stick of the stand into the hole on the back of the backboard.

Assembling & Finishing

7 **Drill into the wooden balls.** Make a 1/4" (6mm) deep hole with your 5/16" (8mm) drill bit in the wooden balls.

8 **Paint as desired.** Refer to page 145 for painting instructions.

9 **Insert the dowels.** Apply glue to the holes you've drilled in the backboard and to the tip of the dowels where the wooden balls will go. Using a wooden mallet, gently tap the ball onto the dowel, then tap the dowel into the hole.

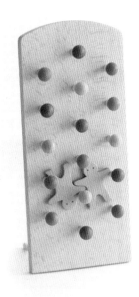

Climbing Toy: UFO

Balance   Move   Repeat

A nostalgic toy that even adults can play with by pulling the string alternately from left to right. Little by little, the UFO will return to the star. Feel free to create a different motif and think of a story.

▶ **Drawing/Pattern: page 154**

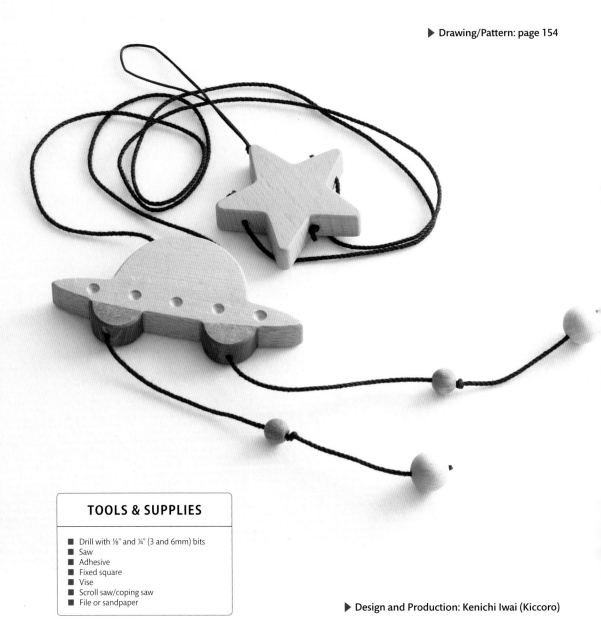

TOOLS & SUPPLIES

- Drill with ⅛" and ¼" (3 and 6mm) bits
- Saw
- Adhesive
- Fixed square
- Vise
- Scroll saw/coping saw
- File or sandpaper

▶ **Design and Production: Kenichi Iwai (Kiccoro)**

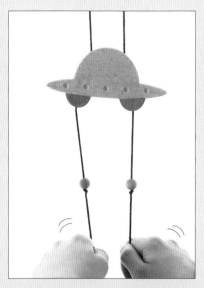

If you pull the string alternately, the UFO climbs up. The trick is to pull the strings slightly inward.

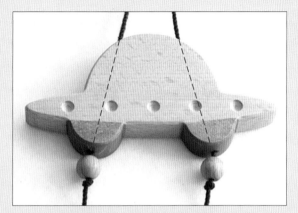

The reason why it moves like this is because the mark is in the shape of a square. This is also key when making other versions of this toy.

IF YOU ARE CAREFUL MAKING YOUR HOLES, IT SHOULD BE EASY TO THREAD THE STRING THROUGH.

When drilling the V-shaped hole, make sure to pay close attention. Once drilled, all that is left is to thread the string. To create the V shape, the hole for the string should be drilled at an angle. Instead of tilting the drill, fix the wood at an angle to make drilling easier. To make the UFO climb up the strings, pull the left and right strings alternately.

Materials Used

Stars and UFO boards are made of European beech. Use materials of the same thickness throughout so it is easy to pass the string through. A ⅛" (3mm) hole needs to be drilled, so avoid using a material that is too thin. Instead of a wooden ball, you can use any shape you like, such as a cube.

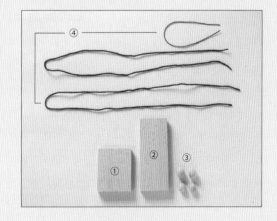

1. **Star:** material of 2⅝" x 2¾" (68mm x 70mm), thickness ⁹⁄₁₆" (15mm)
2. **UFO:** material: about 2⅜" x 4¾" (60 x 120mm), thickness ⁹⁄₁₆" (15mm)
3. **Four wooden balls:** two with ⅜" (10mm) diameter, two about ⁹⁄₁₆" (15mm) in diameter (you can choose the size as you like)
4. **String:** one piece of 15¾" (40cm) and two pieces of 35½" (90cm) with a thickness of ¹⁄₁₆" (1.5mm) to ³⁄₃₂" (2.5mm)
5. **Edge material for drilling guide**

Make a Hole for String

1 Draw the UFO design on the wood. Copy the provided pattern onto the wood.

2 Draw a line. Using a square, draw a straight line perpendicular to the face of the star-shaped wood at the upper end of the guideline. Mark the center point of the line.

How to use the square.

3 Draw the UFO drilling guidelines. To create an inverted *V*-shaped hole for the UFO, drill the hole vertically. Make a 21-degree guide to ensure the hole is at the correct angle.

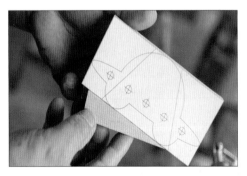

Adjust the angle of the guide so that the drilling line is vertical.

4 Drill into the UFO. Place the UFO blank on the guide made in the previous step. Then, drill a ⅛" (3mm) hole while inserting and withdrawing the drill little by little.

Tip

Be careful not to deviate with the blade when cutting all the way through the board at once. Alternatively, if you cut out the shape, even if the blade doesn't go all the way through, you'll still have a hole.

Use a drill bit that is a little longer than the depth to be drilled.

Drill a hole vertically.

5 Create the stars. Create three star-shaped parts along the guideline. Make a ⅛" (3mm) hole perpendicular to each star-shaped part.

6 Make the handles. Drill through holes about ⅛" (3mm) in diameter in the four wooden balls, which will serve as handles.

Tip

Drilling a hole in the wooden ball for the handle is a little difficult because it rolls easily. Use a vise or similar to hold it still.

Shaping

7 Cut out UFO and star shapes along the lines. At this time, make sure that the hole for the string has gone all the way though the board.

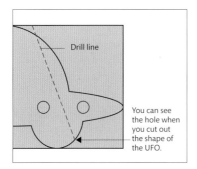

Drill line

You can see the hole when you cut out the shape of the UFO.

8 Drill the windows. Drill a window pattern on the UFO part using a ¼" (6mm) drill bit. Adjust the depth of the hole as desired.

9 Chamfer the edges. Chamfer the edges of the UFO and star parts to make them smooth. Then file them until they become flat.

Finish

10 Paint as desired. See page 145 for instructions.

11 Tie the ball knots. Fold the short string in half and pass it through the hole in the star, making sure that the crease is on top. Then tie a ball knot once at the top and bottom of the string to secure it in place.

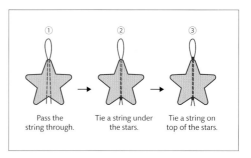

① Pass the string through. ② Tie a string under the stars. ③ Tie a string on top of the stars.

Tip
Reinforce the knot by tying it with a little glue on your finger.

12 Finish the toy. Pass two long strings through the holes on the left and right sides of the star and then tie them at the top. After passing the UFO, move the two small wooden balls that serve as handles to the left. Pass the strings through them to the right and tie a knot under each wooden ball. Next, pass the two wooden balls through the strings and tie a knot at the bottom. This completes the toy.

Merry-Go-Round

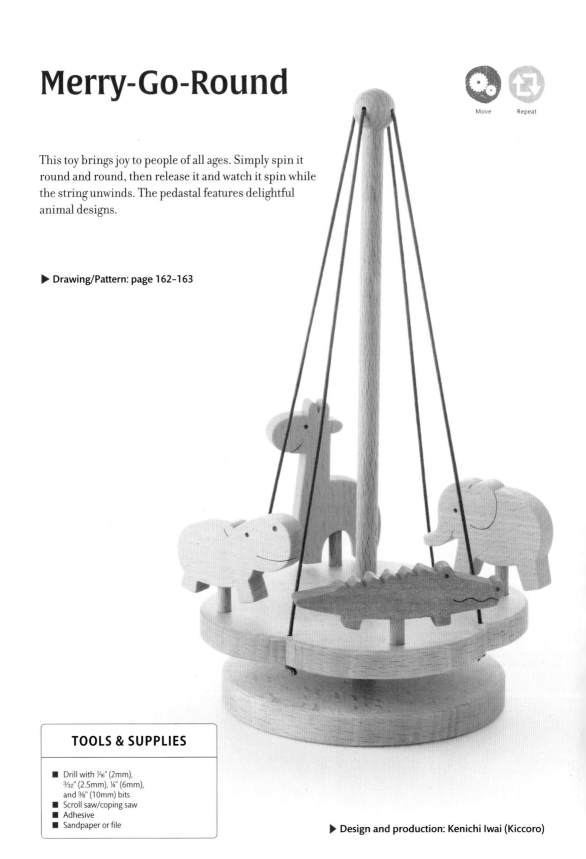

Move   Repeat

This toy brings joy to people of all ages. Simply spin it round and round, then release it and watch it spin while the string unwinds. The pedastal features delightful animal designs.

▶ Drawing/Pattern: page 162–163

TOOLS & SUPPLIES

- Drill with ¹⁄₁₆" (2mm), ³⁄₃₂" (2.5mm), ¼" (6mm), and ³⁄₈" (10mm) bits
- Scroll saw/coping saw
- Adhesive
- Sandpaper or file

▶ Design and production: Kenichi Iwai (Kiccoro)

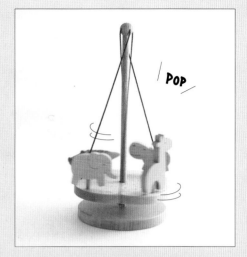

Turn the pedestal and wrap the string around the stick.

Release the string to start the merry-go-round. It creates a soothing and mesmerizing effect as it quietly rotates.

DRILLING HOLES FOR WOODEN BALLS AND SPINNING BOARD

Be careful when drilling holes in the wooden ball and rotating platform. Arrange the holes horizontally and evenly. Hang the rotating platform from the holes in the wooden ball atop the rod. Thread the four strings through the hole and tighten. The key is to arrange them sensibly. Though there are many parts, they can be connected to the string if aligned properly. It can be assembled using only adhesive.

Materials Used

A ¼" (6mm) hole needs to be drilled in the animal parts to attach them to the dowel, so please avoid using materials that are too thin. Additionally, when selecting the material for the string, keep in mind that it will be tied with a ball knot to fix it, so the thickness should be appropriate. I recommend using waxed cord.

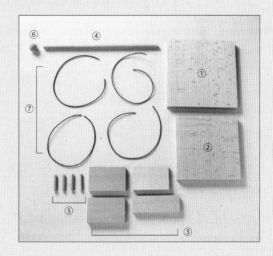

1. **Pedestal:** 4 ¾" x 4 ¾" (120 x 120mm), ½" (13mm) thick board (European beech)
2. **Rotating platform:** Wood board of about 5 ½" x 5 ½" (140 x 140mm), thickness of about ½" (12mm)
3. **Animals**
   Giraffe: 2 ¾" x 1 ¾" (70 x 45mm), ⅜" (10mm) thick
   Crocodile: one 1 ³⁄₁₆" x 3 ⁹⁄₁₆" (30 x 90mm) board, ⅜" (10mm) thick
   Elephant/Hippopotamus: one 1 ¾" x 2 ¾" (45 x 70mm) board, ⅜" (10mm) thick
4. **Center shaft round bar:** dowels with ⅜ dia. (10mm); length of 9 ⁷⁄₁₆" (240mm)
5. **Round bar (x 4):** dowels with ¼" (6mm), length 1 ³⁄₁₆" (30mm)
6. **Wood ball:** ¹¹⁄₁₆" (18mm) in diameter
7. **String (x 4):** about 9 ⅞" (250mm) long, thickness around ¹⁄₁₆" (1.5-2mm)

Pedestal and Rotating Platform

1 **Cut out the pedestal and rotating platform.** Follow the provided pattern to do so.

2 **Drill a hole in the base.** Drill a hole with a diameter of ³⁄₈" (10mm) and a depth of ³⁄₈" (10mm) in the center of the base.

3 **Drill a through hole in the platform.** For the rotating platform, make a through hole with a diameter of ⁷⁄₁₆" (10.5mm) in the center and four through holes with a diameter of ¹⁄₁₆" (2mm) around the perimeter, evenly spaced and ⁵⁄₁₆" (8mm) deep, using a ¹⁄₄" (6mm) drill bit.

Animal Preparation

4 **Trace the patterns.** Trace the animal patterns onto the board you will cut them from.

5 **Attach dowels to the animals.** Attach a round bar or dowel to the lower body part of each animal cutout. Drill a ¹⁄₂" (12mm) deep hole with a ¹⁄₄" (6mm) diameter for insertion. Be sure to measure the depth of the hole accurately.

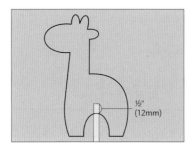

½"
(12mm)

Tip

To prevent the material from becoming unstable, ensure that the shape of the hole is maintained before making any cuts.

6 **Cut out the animals.** Cut out the animal shapes and add eyes, if desired. Drill a ¹⁄₁₆" (2mm) hole for finishing. If cutting small details is difficult, drawing and painting the shapes may be an alternative. Refer to page 145 for instructions on painting.

Preparing the Wooden Ball

7 **Drill into the wooden ball.** Drill a hole that is ¹⁄₃₂" (1mm) deep and ³⁄₈" (10mm) in diameter in the wooden ball to insert the central rod.

8 **Drill holes for strings.** To connect the wooden ball to the platform, drill four holes that are ³⁄₃₂" (2.5mm) in diameter on the face of the ball so that they pass through to the hole drilled in step 7. The position of the holes should be below the center of the ball, and make sure that the two pairs of holes are at right angles to each other.

Make a hole for the string through the side of the wooden ball.

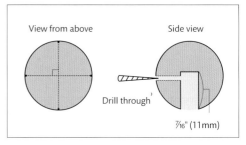

View from above   Side view

Drill through

⁷⁄₁₆" (11mm)

Drill four holes on the wooden ball, evenly spaced and at right angles to each other, as shown in the figure on the left. Make sure the holes are slightly below the center of the sphere, so that they align with the hole drilled in step 7, as shown in the figure on the right.

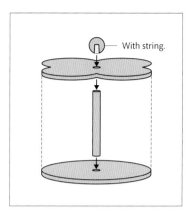
With string.

Finishing / Assembly

9 Chamfer edges. Chamfer the edges of the base, rotating platform, and animal cutouts. You can use a file or sandpaper for this.

10 Insert dowels. Glue the dowels into the animal cutouts.

11 Pass the strings through the ball. Insert each string into one of the four holes in the wooden ball. Once they have passed through, tie a knot in each so it can't slip back out.

Tie a knot.

> **Tip**
> Reinforce the knots with a little glue.

12 Assemble. Assemble the base, central shaft, rotating platform, and wooden ball (with string) in that order. Hold the rotating platform at the desired height and pass the strings through its holes, then tie a knot on the back of the platform while adjusting its position for balance. Pay careful attention to get the string tension equally distributed. Make sure to cut any excess string after tying the knot.

13 Glue the wooden ball. Glue the wooden ball to the central shaft. Once dried, the project is complete.

Tie the string in a knot on the back of the rotating platform. Be careful not to let the knot come loose.

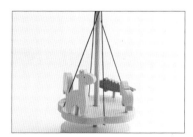

Merry-Go-Round (Kiccoro)

Katakata Doll (Kiccoro)

Climbing Toy: UFO (Kiccoro)

Dog Pull Toy

Balance Move

When you pull the string, the wooden dog will follow you and walk along with you. It's adorable how it sways a little bit as it moves forward. You can play with it while sitting or walking, simply by pulling the string.

▶ Drawing/Pattern: page 153

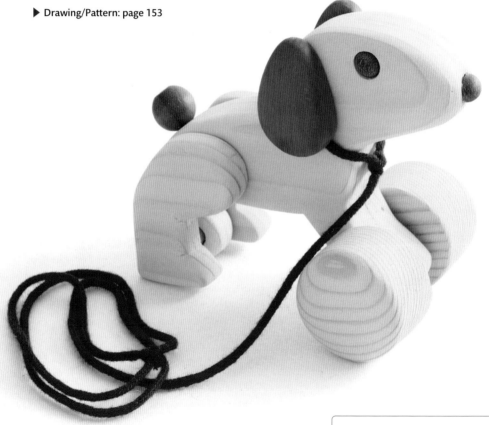

TOOLS & SUPPLIES

- ■ Drill with ¼" (6mm), ⅜" (10mm), and ⁷⁄₁₆" (11mm) bits
- ■ Saw
- ■ Scroll saw/coping saw
- ■ Carving knife
- ■ Clamps
- ■ Adhesive
- ■ Sandpaper or file

▶ Design and Production: Yutaka Ito (Comomg)

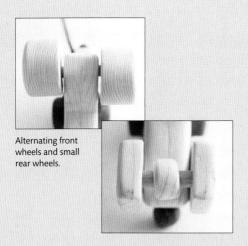

Alternating front wheels and small rear wheels.

It wobbles with perfect balance.

ASSEMBLING WITH DOWELS AND ADHESIVE FOR A SMOOTH FORM

The main focus of this project is on assembling the parts using dowels and adhesive to achieve a smooth form. The dog's body parts are made by gluing two pieces of material together and drilling holes for the dowels without penetrating through. The wheels are also cut from wood, with careful attention to creating clean, smooth discs that are soft to the touch. Finally, polish the pieces to finish.

Materials Used

All dowels used for assembly are the same size as the main body. The body is made of Ezo spruce, while the ears are made of cherry wood to create shading effects.

1. **Main body, rear legs, rear wheels:** material of about 5 $^{15}/_{16}$" x 17$^{3}/_{4}$" (150 x 450mm), thickness $^{9}/_{16}$" (15mm)
2. **Front wheels (x 2):** wood with 1 $^{3}/_{16}$" (30mm) thickness
3. **Ears:** wood with a thickness of ½" (12mm)
4. **Axle:** $^{3}/_{8}$" (10mm). For front wheels: 2" (50mm) long board. For rear wheels: 1 $^{9}/_{16}$" (40mm) long board
5. **Round bar for dowels (9 pieces):** ¼" (6mm) diameter, 2" (50mm) long
6. **Eyes, nose:** Wood ball (x3), ½" (12mm)
7. **Tail:** wooden ball, $^{11}/_{16}$" (18mm) diameter
8. **Strap:** leather, 31 ½" (80cm) long (adjust as desired)

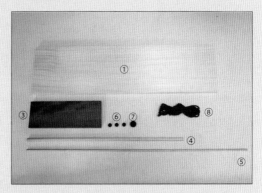

*Not all materials.

Drilling and Cutting

1 **Transfer the shape of the paper pattern onto the material.** For the main body and rear legs, flip the paper pattern and cut out the symmetrical parts. Create one pair at a time. The ears and front wheels are identical, so create two of them.

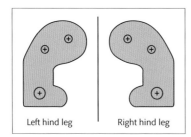

Left hind leg   Right hind leg

2 **Create holes for the legs and wheels.** Before cutting out the shape, create holes for the rear wheels and front legs of the main body in addition to the existing holes. Ensure that the holes do not penetrate through the material. Carefully follow the markings on the pattern and drill holes accordingly.

3 **Create the tail.** Drill a ¼" (6mm) hole ⁵⁄₁₆" (8mm) deep into one of the wooden balls to create the tail.

4 **Cut out each part.** For this, use a coping saw. Aim to make the cuts as vertical as possible.

Tip

Keep the wood and the saw blade vertical as you cut.

Do not tilt the saw blade back and forth or left and right.

5 **Drill holes.** Drill holes in the appropriate spots on both sides of the main body. Make sure the holes don't go all the way through. Glue the parts together and use clamps to hold everything until the adhesive dries.

Part Surface Finish

6 **Cut out the parts.** Use a scroll saw to roughly cut the shapes, and then refine them with a knife for precision. Smooth out the left and right edges of the rear wheel, the edges of the front wheel, the rear legs, and the surface where the ear holes are not drilled (the outer surface).

7 **Sand the pieces.** Use sandpaper to smooth out any roughness or unevenness caused by the coping saw and knife marks.

Tip

To create the front and rear wheels, cut out the desired shape from the sheet material. Start by cutting a rough straight line around the outer edge of the pattern paper. Then, use a knife or sandpaper to smooth out any polygonal corners. If you have a round bar of the same size, you can also use that as a substitute for the wheels.

Cut roughly along a straight line.

Correct the outline with a knife.

Smooth it with sandpaper.

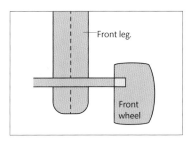

By deliberately not aligning the heights, the legs move forward while swaying as they roll.

10 **Attach the second front wheel.** Apply adhesive to the hole in the other front wheel part and align it with the first front wheel so that they are symmetrical. Attach the second front wheel to the axle in a manner that is different from the first front wheel, ensuring that they are securely connected. Pay attention to the alignment and positioning to achieve a balanced and symmetrical appearance but be sure to install the wheels at different heights to give the toy it's wobbly movement.

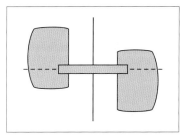

8 **Cut the holes for the nose and tail.** Referencing the drawing (page 153), carefully cut out the holes for the nose and tail in the assembled body. Ensure that the cuts are precise and follow the designated markings.

Front Wheel Assembly

9 **Attach the first front wheel.** Apply adhesive to the hole in one of the front wheel parts. Once the adhesive is applied, insert the axle for the front wheel into the hole and pass it through the corresponding hole in the front leg of the body part. Make sure the axle fits securely and the front wheel is properly aligned with the front leg.

Rear Wheel Assembly

11 **Drill dowel holes on either side of the rear leg part.** Apply glue to the two places where the dowels will be inserted, as well as to the axle holes. Attach the dowels and the axle for the rear wheel, ensuring a secure connection. The adhesive will help hold the components together and provide stability.

12 **Attach a dowel to the first rear leg.** Apply adhesive to the dowel hole on the rear leg of the main body part. Attach the dowel and pass it through the rear wheel part. The adhesive will help secure the connection and ensure stability between the main body and the rear wheel.

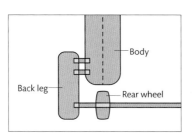

13 **Attach a dowel to the second rear leg.** Insert dowels in the other rear leg part in the same way and attach it to the main body part.

Finishing Touches

14 **Attach the ears.** Apply adhesive to the holes of the ear parts and the corresponding holes on the body parts. Insert dowels into the ear parts and attach them securely to the body. Ensure that the dowels are inserted fully into the holes for a strong and stable connection. The adhesive will help bond the parts together firmly.

15 **Attach the eyes and nose.** Apply glue to the holes designated for the eyes and nose on the body parts. Then, carefully insert a wooden ball with a diameter of ½" (12mm) into each hole. Ensure that the wooden balls are fully inserted and secure in place. The glue will help hold the wooden balls firmly in position.

16 **Attach the tail.** For the tail, apply glue to the hole in the wooden ball, which was prepared in step 3, and to the corresponding hole on the main body part. Insert the dowel into the wooden ball and firmly attach it in place.

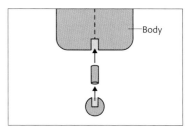

17 **Make the leash.** Wrap the string around the neck of the main body part and tie it, and then tie it on the handle side to make a loop.

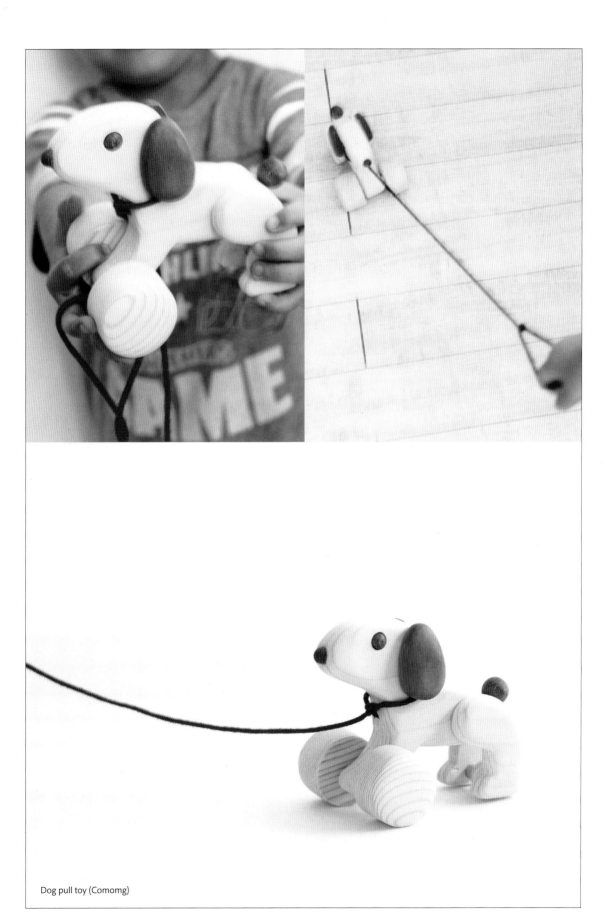

Dog pull toy (Comomg)

Seesaw

Balance   Move

Gently place animals on the seesaw. Which one should you move to make it tilt left or right?

▶ Drawing/Pattern: pages 160–161

TOOLS & SUPPLIES

- Drill with ⅟₃₂" (1mm) bit
- Short knife
- Scroll saw/coping saw
- Adhesive
- Paint (your choice)
- Sandpaper or file

▶ **Design/Production: Atsuko Miyazaki (Comomg)**

Move the animals around the seesaw. Where should you put the animal next time?

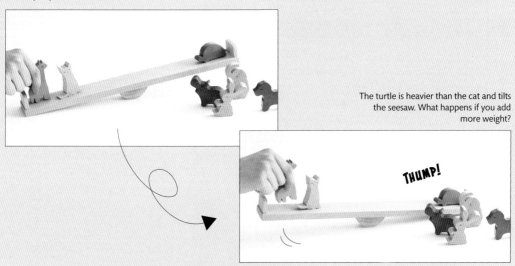

The turtle is heavier than the cat and tilts the seesaw. What happens if you add more weight?

THUMP!

FINISHING DETAILS

The idea behind this toy is simple, so let's concentrate on giving the animals a polished look. The base is quite easy to assemble, so feel free to give it a go. You and your child can enjoy displaying it proudly. When crafting the animal parts by hand, strive for a smooth and clean finish. Moreover, since this toy allows for various dimensions and shapes, you can mix and match to create your own unique designs. Let your creativity flow and have fun telling stories with your creations.

Materials Used

In this project, beech wood is used for both the seesaw table and the animal parts. When cutting out the animal shapes, you can use the tools that are available to you. If possible, working with larger pieces of wood will make the process easier.

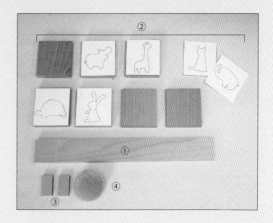

1. **Seesaw stand:** 1 ⁹⁄₁₆" x 14" (40mm x 350mm) wood board with a thickness of ⅜" (10mm)
2. **Animal parts:** 2 ¾" x 2 ¾" (70 x 70mm) boards with a thickness of about ⁵⁄₁₆"–⅜" (8–10mm)
3. **Both ends:** ¼" x ¾" x 1 ⅜" (6 x 20 x 35mm)
4. **Fulcrum:** dowel approximately 2" (50mm) in diameter

Cut Out Parts

1 Prepare the seesaw base and both ends. Cut them out according to the given dimensions. Consider adding a slight curve to the left and right if desired.

2 Cut the fulcrum. Cut a semicircular fulcrum from a round bar or dowel, creating a base of 2" (50mm), height of ¾" (20mm), and thickness of 1 ³/₁₆" (30mm). Don't fret too much over the shape, as it doesn't need to be a perfect semicircle. Small variations in dimensions are acceptable and won't cause any issues.

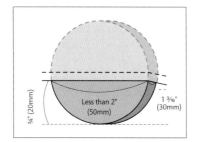

¾" (20mm)   Less than 2" (50mm)   1 ³/₁₆" (30mm)

Cut into slightly smaller than half circles.

3 Prepare the animal parts. Cut out the animal parts and use a drill to create eye holes, if desired.

Insert the blade in the direction indicated by the arrow when cutting the marked part in the photo. Ensure the material and blade are kept vertical.

Tip

If you find it difficult to cut the curved lines of the animal parts with your coping saw, first cut out the outlines with straight lines.

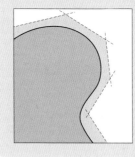

If you cut along the original outline as much as possible, finishing the cuts in step 4 will be easier.

Smooth the Pieces

4 Smooth the pieces. Use sandpaper or a file to shape and smooth the sides and surfaces of all the materials. Pay special attention to the corners, ensuring that the thread surface is also smoothed to prevent any roughness that could be uncomfortable to touch.

Address any marks and unevenness left by the coping saw blade. If there are multiple corners remaining, carefully trim them using a small knife before filing them to achieve a smooth finish.

5 **Paint the pieces (optional).** Use child-safe paints to add color according to your preferences. For tips on painting techniques, please refer to page 145.

6 **Attach the fulcrum.** Glue the fulcrum part to the center of the base at the bottom. At the ends of the base, center two pieces of wood as pictured.

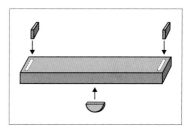

Tip

Find the center of gravity and the left/right balance by carefully placing the fulcrum at the center and positioning both ends accordingly.

Tip

Achieve neat finishes on flat and straight parts by wrapping sandpaper around wood scraps. For parts with many curves, fold the sandpaper into three sections to make it more manageable. Start with a lower grit and coarser mesh (around 180 to 240) to achieve smoothness. If you need to reshape the outline, or create more roundness, begin with 80 grit. Once the desired shape is established with a rougher grit like 120, fine-tune the surface using finer grits.

Train

This wooden train is designed with leather joints, allowing you to easily modify its shape and transform it into different vehicles. Whether it becomes a car, a truck, or something entirely new, the versatility of this toy sparks creativity. Crafted with the beauty and warmth of wood, it offers a delightful tactile experience and ages gracefully with time. Take pleasure in the natural texture and charm of this wooden train, ensuring hours of enjoyment for children and adults alike.

Move

▶ Drawing/Pattern: page 155

▶ Design and Production: Kuniaki Kishi
   (Furniture Studio Acloge Furniture)

TOOLS & SUPPLIES

- ■ Drill with ⅟₁₆" (1.5mm), ³⁄₁₆" (5mm), ¼" (6mm), ½" (12mm), and ⁹⁄₁₆" (15mm) bits
- ■ Chisel
- ■ Leather strips (attach hook for connection)
- ■ Hooks
- ■ Router (straight bit ⁵⁄₁₆" (8mm) / round face bit 2R/roller bit)
- ■ Circular saw
- ■ Scroll saw/coping saw
- ■ Hook punch
- ■ Leather punch
- ■ Sandpaper or file
- ■ Mallet
- ■ Hammer
- ■ Screwdriver
- ■ Clamps

The connection between the cars is of the hook type, where hooks on one car latch onto hooks on another. The use of leather for the connections adds a pleasant texture that blends well with the wood.

SNAP!

If you create multiple central cars, the articulated train can become endlessly long.

CREATE A SIMPLE DESIGN THAT IS BEAUTIFULLY CRAFTED.

Drill a bearing hole in the main body and attach an axle and a wheel. Keeping it simple is key, as the focus should be on material selection and finishing. Give it a try and aim for a polished look. As a unique feature of the train model, we will create a connecting part. Although the model is designed as a three-car formation, you can connect even more cars, if desired.

If you have access to a router or a circular saw, you can create a jig to streamline the process of making multiple pieces with the same shape. This jig will help ensure consistency and efficiency in your woodworking project.

Materials Used

For the main body and wheels of the train, it is recommended to use finely grained wood that does not have a rough grain. In this manual, three different types of wood with varying colors are used for the body. While some of these may be difficult to obtain, you can try looking for similar materials at specialized stores or craft stores.

To create the joint, you will need leather and hooks. It is recommended to use two sets of hooks per connection point. Additionally, you will require wood screws to attach the hooks to the main body. Please note that attaching the hooks will require special tools such as a hook punch and a leather punch to punch holes in the leather. Make sure to prepare these tools accordingly. You can find these tools and materials at craft stores and specialized shops.

1. **Body:** ¾" (20mm) thick board (black walnut, maple, mountain cherry).
2. **Wheel:** ¾" (20 to 22mm) round bar (black walnut).
3. **Axle:** ³⁄₁₆" (5mm) round bar (Sapele)
4. **Links**
   Leather (soft): Hook, ½" (12mm)
   Wood screw (head diameter a little less than
      ³⁄₁₆" [5mm]), shaft diameter a little more than
      ¹⁄₁₆" (2mm), length about ½" (12mm))

You can find leather and hooks for the joints at craft stores. The hook mounting tools needed for attaching the hooks are also available at these stores.

Make the Body

1 **Trim and cut the main body.** Trim the height of the main body to a measurement of 1¹¹⁄₁₆" (43mm). Then, cut it to a 3⁹⁄₁₆" (90mm) length.

2 **Mark the window's spot.** Using a chisel or a drill, carefully copy the position of the window onto the main body. Begin by making rough cuts to shape the interior of the window. Refer to Drawing A on page 155 (specifically the center) for the window's position and Drawing C for guidance on the overall vehicle shape.

After cutting the main body along the direction of the woodgrain, proceed to make horizontal cuts to achieve the precise dimensions required.

3 **Cut out the window.** Using a router with an ⁵⁄₁₆" (8mm) wide straight bit, carefully shape and finish the window. You can use a jig to make this easier, if you'd like.

4 **Cut the front of the body.** Diagonally cut off the front upper part of the body.

How to use the jig is explained in the sidebar on the right.

※ Medium-Density Fiberboard (MDF) is a type of engineered wood made by compressing plant fibers with a resin binder. It offers a consistent density and smooth surface, commonly used in woodworking and construction.

Make a Train Car Window Jig

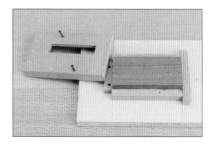

❶ Attach a ⅜" (10mm) square lumber to a sturdy board to create a frame that securely holds the vehicle body in place. Use screws to firmly secure the corners of the frame.

❷ Use a ³⁄₁₆" (5mm) thick board (such as MDF) to create a cover that will go on top of the frame. Attach the cover using square lumber in the same manner as in Step 1. Cut out a rectangle measuring ⁹⁄₁₆" x 2 ½" (15 x 66mm) for the central car—at the designated position for the window on the cover.

❸ Secure the wooden body of the car to the frame and cover it with the lid. If the lid doesn't fit snugly on the wood, make necessary adjustments by trimming the squares.

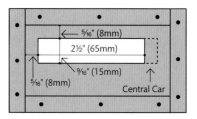

⁵⁄₁₆" (8mm)
2½" (65mm)
⁹⁄₁₆" (15mm)
⁵⁄₁₆" (8mm)
Central Car

❹ When using the train, place two lids in a way that ensures they stay in place and do not come off. Secure them using wood screws to hold the desired position.

Tip

I'll show you two methods to achieve the desired window shape without using a router. The first method involves using a chisel to hollow out the inside after rough shaving. The second method is to create a semicircular edge for the window and drill it with a 9/16" (15mm) drill. Both methods require chiseling for refinement, but if you don't have a router, the latter method is recommended as it produces a beautiful curve.

Instead of using a router to scrape the outside, carefully scrape the surface little by little with a chisel. Make sure to securely fix the body in place with a clamp while working on it.

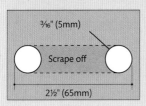

Drill holes at both ends of the window, and then use a coping saw or chisel to carefully remove the material between the holes, creating a clean gap.

³⁄₁₆" (5mm)
Scrape off
2½" (65mm)

5 Soften the edges. Chamfer all edges with sandpaper.

Tip

To maintain a consistent angle when using a circular saw, you can use a guide to ensure uniform cuts. This allows you to achieve consistent shapes every time. Additionally, if you need to create two leading cars, you can clamp them together and cut them simultaneously to ensure the angles are aligned.

Create a wooden frame to hold down the material from two directions and use it as a guide.

6 Drill holes. Drill three holes on the bottom of the project to embed the hooks. Start by drilling the holes gradually, following the dimensions indicated in Drawing B. Refer to the provided figure for the specific shape of the holes.

Tip

If you have a router available, you can use a 2R round bit to shape the side corners and a roller bit for the other corners and the inside of the window. This will give you a clean chamfered edge. After the initial cut, you may notice that the top and bottom of the piece are not perfectly at right angles. In that case, you can use sandpaper to carefully sand and shape those areas until they are smooth and aligned.

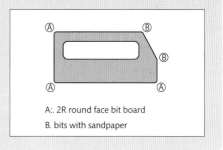

A:. 2R round face bit board
B. bits with sandpaper

7 Drill a hole for the axle. Drill a hole for the axle using a ³⁄₁₆" (5mm) drill bit. Refer to Drawing A on page 155 for the exact position.

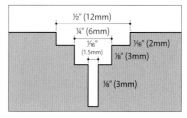

In the first stage, use a drill bit with a diameter of ½" (12mm) to create holes that are ¹⁄₁₆" (2mm) deep. In the second stage, use a drill bit with a diameter of ¼" (6mm) to create holes that are ⅛" (3mm) deep. In the third stage, use a drill bit with a diameter of ¹⁄₁₆" (2mm) to create holes that are ³⁄₈" (10mm) deep. The first and second stage holes are intended for the hooks, while the third stage holes serve as pilot holes for the screws.

8 **Cut out the wheels.** Cut the round bar into ³⁄₈" (10mm)-wide round slices to create four wheels.

Wheels and Axles

9 **Drill a hole in the center.** Drill a ³⁄₁₆" (5mm), ¼" (6mm) deep hole in the center open.

10 **Chamfer the edges.** Use a file or sandpaper.

11 **Cut out the axles.** Cut out two axles with a length of 1⁵⁄₁₆" (30mm).

12 **Cut the leather strips.** Cut out the leather to about ⁹⁄₁₆" x 1³⁄₄" (15 x 45mm). Soft leather can be cut with scissors.

Connecting Parts

13 **Trace the pattern.** On the cut-out leather, trace the outline and hole positions from the pattern shown on page 87.

14 **Punch holes.** Use a leather punch to punch holes in the leather at the indicated positions.

15 **Attach the hooks.** Pass the hooks through the holes and fix them in place.

16 **Cut the leather strips.** Cut out the outline from the pattern according to the template.

17 **Sand the parts.** Sand the surface of all parts with sandpaper. Apply a nontoxic finish, if desired.

Surface Finish

18 **Apply a finish.** Apply a coat of clear paint to the entire surface and allow it to dry. This will provide a protective finish. Alternatively, you can choose to finish it by applying vegetable oil, which can enhance the natural beauty of the wood. Ensure the oil is evenly applied and allow it to penetrate the wood before wiping off any excess. This will provide a smooth and polished finish.

19 **Glue on a wheel.** Glue one wheel to one side of an axle.

Assembly

20 **Insert the axle.** Pass the axle through the hole in the main body, then glue on the other wheel. Do this for both sets of wheels.

Tip

To create a gap between the wheels and the main body, place a blank of approximately 1/32" (1mm) thickness (any suitable material will work) between one side of the wheel and the main body. This will result in a gap of 0.5mm on each side. Ensure that the wheels are positioned properly and can freely rotate without any interference. Allow the adhesive to dry completely while the blank is in place to maintain the desired gap. Once the adhesive is dry, remove the blank and verify that the wheels can move smoothly.

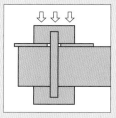

To stabilize the axle, insert a material of approximately 1/32" (1mm) thickness between the wheel and the body. This will help secure the shaft by applying pressure from both sides. Insert the axle all the way through, ensuring it is properly aligned and positioned within the designated holes. The added material will provide stability and prevent any excessive movement of the axle.

Pattern for leather cutouts (actual size).

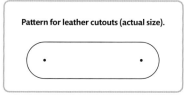

21 **Glue the rings.** Apply glue to the ring and insert it into the predrilled hole in the body, ensuring a secure and snug fit. The ring will serve as a connection point for the hook, allowing it to be attached firmly. Make sure the ring is properly aligned with the hook attachment point. Allow the glue to dry thoroughly, ensuring a strong bond between the ring and the body.

Tip

Also attach the other side of the hook, which receives the protrusion. While the original attachment method involves hooking it as before, in this case, it is secured using a screw since it is attached to a hole in the wooden body.

Align the receiving side of the hook with the corresponding hole in the wooden body. Insert a screw through the hole in the hook and tighten it securely using a screwdriver. This ensures a stable and secure connection between the hook and the wooden body.

By using this method, the hook will be firmly attached to the wooden body, allowing for a reliable and durable joint.

Fit the hook into the stepped hole and secure it with a screw. Ensure that the screw head is smaller than the recess of the hook for proper fixation. Use a thin screwdriver for tightening.

22 **Check the hook.** Check that the hook can be fastened. If so, you're all done!

Exercise caution during the installation of the hook to prevent crushing, as it can lead to inadequate fastening or potential detachment.

Seesaw (Comomg).

Train (Furniture Studio Acroge Furniture).

Rainbow Puzzle

Rainbow-colored discs of various sizes make up this puzzle. Match each disc to its corresponding dimple of the same color and size. Use high-quality materials and strive for a refined finish to enhance its overall aesthetic.

Color Matching

Shape Matching

▶ Drawing/Pattern: page 152

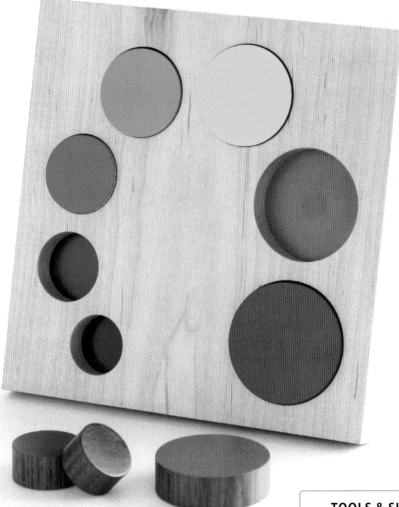

TOOLS & SUPPLIES

- Forstner bit sizes: 1 ³⁄₁₆" (30mm), 1 ³⁄₈" (35mm), 1 ⁹⁄₁₆" (40mm), 1¾ (45mm), 2" (50mm), 2 ³⁄₁₆" (55mm), 2³⁄₈" (60mm)
- Drill bit sizes: ¹⁄₁₆" (2.5mm), ³⁄₁₆" (5mm), ½" (12mm)
- Paint (seven colors and a clearcoat)
- Router
- Masking tape
- Saw
- Scroll saw/coping saw
- Drill
- Sandpaper or file
- Lathe
- Planer

▶ **Design and Production: Kuniaki Kishi**
   (Furniture Studio Acloge Furniture)

PLUNK!

Insert each disc into its corresponding dimple based on color and size, creating a satisfying tactile experience.

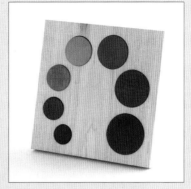

The back of the disc is subtly enhanced with the natural woodgrain, adding an elegant touch.

ACHIEVE A COMFORTABLE TEXTURE BY FINE-TUNING THE DIAMETER OF THE DISC

Ensure a snug fit by adjusting the size of the holes and discs. If they are too tight, carefully scrape the sides of the disc to create a diameter of approximately ³/₁₆" (5mm), creating a slight gap. Fine-tune the adjustment so that the discs can be smoothly inserted and removed, providing a comfortable experience. Pay attention to the hole size, which should be large enough for easy manipulation. Instead of a regular drill bit, consider using a Forstner bit for a refined texture. While the project suggests using 7 types of high-grade wood in round bar form, feel free to explore alternative materials if they are more accessible. If you have a lathe, you have the flexibility to utilize any combination of materials that you prefer.

It may be difficult to obtain all seven types of lumber, but it is worth the challenge.

This Forstner bit is 2 ³/₈" (60mm) and can be purchased for around $10.

Materials Used

The disc protrudes ¹/₁₆" (2mm) from the body with a thickness of ⁹/₁₆" (15mm), when assembled. You can adjust the disc thickness if the body is not ⁹/₁₆" (15mm) thick. If you find discounted lumber with suitable discs, use this method. The back board is independent of the structure, so thickness variations are not an issue. For material, maple is recommended for its workability and texture. If using solid wood, painting over it won't affect the wood's color. Choose a paint type that doesn't require surface finishing, but follow the instructions and notes provided for your specific paint.

* Not all materials

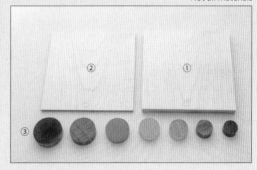

1. **Main body**
   ⁹/₁₆" (15mm) thick board (maple)
   Size: 7 ⁷/₈" (200mm) square
2. **Backboard**
   ¼" (6mm)-thick board (maple)
   Size: 7 ½" (190mm) square
3. **Disc**
   Round bar in the following sizes: 1 ³/₁₆" (30mm),
   1 ³/₈" (35mm), 1 ⁹/₁₆" (40mm), 1 ¾" (45mm),
   2" (50mm), 2 ³/₁₆" (55mm), 2 ³/₈" (60mm)

   Material options: Black walnut, teak, mizunara, beech, cherry, yamazakura, sapele mahogany

4. **Stand** ½" (12mm) round bar. Length: 2" (50mm)
5. **Wood screws**
   Quantity: 4
   Head diameter: slightly less than ³/₁₆" (5mm)
   Shaft diameter: slightly over ¹/₁₆" (2mm)
   Length: about ½" (12mm)

Make the Body

1 Prepare the main body. Cut it into a 7⅞" x 7⅞" (200 x 200mm) square shape.

2 Mark the hole's center. Refer to Drawing A (page 152) for the hole position.

> **Tip**
> If you make a paper pattern, it is easy to apply it to the main body and poke the center point with a nail or similar.

3 Drill the holes. Secure a scrap board underneath the main body, then use a bore bit of the appropriate diameter to drill a round hole. Ensure that the hole is drilled vertically and proceed with caution.

4 Smooth the corners. Chamfer all corners of the main body, except for the corner in contact with the back board on the far side of the hole. Use sandpaper or a chamfering tool to give them a smooth and rounded finish.

> **Tip**
> Chamfering can of course be done with a file or planer. However, with a rotary tool and attached sanding drum, you can remove the edges quickly and cleanly.

5 Sand. Smooth the surface with sandpaper.

> **Tip**
> With your sandpapers, gradually progress from 180 to 240 and then to 320 grit to achieve a fine grain and smooth finish. Remember to use water for wiping in between each stage.

6 Prepare for coating. Apply a clear coat to all surfaces, except for the back surface where the backboard is attached.

Make a Backing Board

7 Prepare the back board. Cut it into a square measuring 7½" x 7½" (190 x 190mm) to start with.

8 Chamfer the board. Chamfer all surfaces except for the corners in contact with the main body.

9 Sand the board. As with the main body, finish the surface with sandpaper.

10 Paint the main body. Apply paint to the overlapping areas of the main body holes using seven different colors.

> **Tip**
> Copy the hole positions from the main body onto the back board ensuring that each side is reduced by ³⁄₁₆" (5mm). Take care when aligning and stacking them. Additionally, fill the holes with enough filler to conceal any unpainted areas. Apply a sufficient amount to ensure complete coverage.

11 Add a clear coat. Clear coat the back and sides.

Attach the Main Body and the Back Board

12 **Drill pilot holes.** Drill pilot holes for wood screws in the four corners of the back panel, approximately $^9/_{32}$" (7mm) away from each corner. Use a $^3/_{16}$" (5mm) drill bit and drill to a depth of $^1/_{16}$" (2mm). Additionally, drill a $^3/_{32}$" (2.5mm) through hole in the center. Take care while drilling.

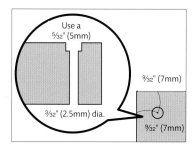

13 **Apply glue to the back board.** Create a $^3/_{16}$" (5mm) step on each side of the circumference of the holes you made in the previous step. Place the backboard in the center of the back of the main body and glue it using industrial glue.

> **Tip**
> Apply a thin and even layer of wood glue so that when the boards are pressed together, the wood glue will not seep into the holes.

14 **Add wood screws.** Attach the backboard securely to the main body by inserting and tightening wood screws at each of the four corners.

15 **Clamp the backing to the main body.** Affix sturdy wooden strips or narrow boards on both sides to clamp the backing firmly to the main body. This will help ensure a tight bond.

> **Tip**
> After affixing the sturdy wooden strips on both sides, ensure that the main body and back panel are cut out to the same size and fit perfectly. Once they are pasted together, you can use a rotary tool to carefully scrape off the steps.

Make a Disc

16 **Cut the discs.** Cut a disc with a thickness of $^{11}/_{16}$" (17mm) each from the required bars.

> **Tip**
> If you have a lathe, you can cut a round bar even from square timber, expanding the range of wood grades you can use.

17 **Size the discs to the holes.** Use paper as a sleeve for easy insertion and removal of the discs. File the sides of each disc until you achieve a snug fit for each hole.

Gradually shape the discs little by little while inserting them into their holes.

> **Tip**
> Carefully and evenly sand the entire surface, ensuring the circular shape is maintained. Once done, place it in the designated area.

18 **Sand the pieces.** Smooth the surface by using sandpaper to remove any imperfections and achieve a refined finish.

Achieve a smooth finish by gently moving the disc over sandpaper attached to a flat board. This will help refine the surface.

19 **Paint the discs.** Apply paint in seven different colors corresponding to the holes of the same size on one side. Repeat the application until the coating is even and there are no visible inconsistencies.

Tip
To prevent paint from getting on the sides, apply masking tape to those areas before painting. Once the paint is dry, carefully sand off any excess paint on the sides to create a smooth and even finish.

20 **Apply a clear coat.** This should go on all areas of the discs aside from the painted surfaces.

Finish

21 **Apply a final clear coat.** Once all paint has dried, apply a clear coat to all parts of the project.

Make a Stand

❶ Drill a ⅜" (10mm) round hole with a depth of ½" (12mm)

❷ Cut a ½" (12mm) dowel to a length of 2" (50mm).

❸ Gently shave the tip to allow for easy insertion into the hole.

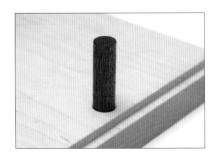

Rainbow Puzzle (Furniture Workshop Acloge Furniture).

Kitchenette

Explore the joy of cooking and pretend dishwashing with our captivating kids' kitchenette. Designed for all children, this playset offers endless imaginative play possibilities. When not in use, it conveniently transforms into a tidy shelf for storing books and toys, keeping the play area organized. Let your little ones unleash their creativity and embark on culinary adventures in their very own kitchenette.

Put Away

Move

▶ Drawing/Pattern: pages 175–177

TOOLS & SUPPLIES

- Drill with ¹⁄₁₆" (2mm), ¼" (6mm), ⁵⁄₁₆" (8mm), ⅜" (10mm), and ¾" (20mm) bits
- Clear coat finish
- Router (straight bit, width ¼" [6mm])
- All-purpose adhesive for attaching metal
- Open up to about 35⁷⁄₁₆" (900mm)
- About 4 F-clamps
- Saw
- Scroll saw/coping saw
- Vise
- Electric sander
- Sandpaper or fil

▶ Design and Production: Masahiro Yano (Ken Rack System)

The faucet and handle actually turn.

The stove knob also moves.

CUSTOMIZE YOUR SHELF: ENDLESS POSSIBILITIES!

In this guide, we'll show you how to create a traditional-style shelf that can be customized to your liking. With a design resembling a kitchen setup, complete with a fixed shelf board and elements like a stove, water supply, and sink, this shelf will provide a perfect workbench for children. It stands at approximately 19¾" (about 50cm) in height, making it accessible for little ones. The assembly primarily involves using glue, but we'll also explore creating a "tongue-and-groove joint," which involves creating grooves with a router and joining the boards for added strength. While this method may be slightly challenging, it guarantees a sturdy and durable finish.

Materials Used

The main material is a ¾" x 11 ¹³/₁₆" (19 x 300mm) board. Laminated pine wood or SPF (Spruce-Pine-Fir) can be used as the material. The specific type of wood is not crucial.

For the faucet or stove knob:

1. You can use various dowels with different thicknesses. As long as they can be installed, suitable substitute materials can be used.

For the sink:

1. A tub of a suitable size can be used. Stainless steel tub of about 7 ⅞" x 9 ⅞" (200 x 250mm) are available at shops.

Additional materials needed:

1. **Veneer for** the back panel
2. **Wood screws** to attach the legs

Round bar materials in various thicknesses:

1. **Stovetop knob:** Round bar with 2" (50mm) dia.
2. **Stopper and faucet stem:** 1³/₁₆" (30mm) round bar
3. **Faucet tip and handle stem:** ¾" (20mm) round bar
4. **Rotating shaft:** ⅜" (10mm) round bar
5. **Dowels:** ¼" (6mm) round bar
6. **You will** also need 18 screws with a diameter of ³/₁₆" (5mm) and a length of 1" (25mm)

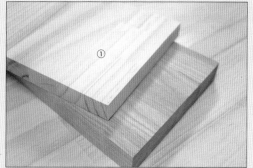

* Not all materials

Cut Out

1 **Cut out all the parts.** Refer to the pattern on page 175–177 for all dimensions.

Tip

The legs are long and slender, so you can use square lumber of similar thicknesses.

2 **Cut out the back piece.** The back is cut from plywood.

Make a Sink

3 **Cut the hole.** Cut out a hole in the top board to make a place for the sink.

Tip

The cutout in the sink should match the size of the tub you are using. Don't forget to make it slightly smaller so that the tub can catch on the edge of the cutout. The next step is to drill a hole for the faucet, which should also be adjusted according to the size of the sink.

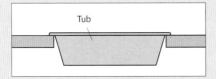

The top board must be cut out large enough to catch the end of the tub.

4 **Create holes for the faucet and handles.** The holes should be roughly ⅜" (10mm) in diameter. Arrange them so they are symmetrical and centered over the sink as pictured.

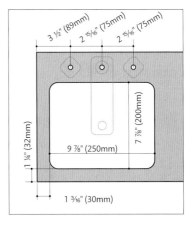

Arrange the faucet parts so that they are symmetrically arranged and placed in the center of the sink.

Make the Stove

5 **Cut out an opening.** Cut out a 4" x 4" (100 x 100mm) opening for the stove. You can decorate the parts with trivets.

Tip

Decorations can be made of wood as shown in the illustration or drawn with a permanent marker.

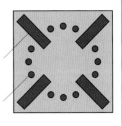

Attach a board measuring ⅜" x 1 ½" (10 x 38mm) and with a thickness of approximately ⅛" (3mm).

Drill holes and fill them with a ¼" (6mm) round bar.

You can arrange the design of the trivet according to your preference.

6 Cut the knob. The stove knob is made from a round bar with a diameter of ³/₁₆" (5mm). Cut it into ½" (12mm) sections or purchase similar-sized discs.

7 Chamfer the knob. Create a chamfer on one side of the knob, while the other side (which will be facing the table) should be rounded with a radius of approximately ³/₁₆" (5mm).

8 Drill a hole for the knob. Drill a hole on the center of the back side, about ³/₈" (10mm) deep, with a diameter of around ⁵/₁₆" (8mm).

9 Create a fixed shaft. Take a ³/₈" (10mm) board and cut it to a length of approximately 1½"(38mm). Attach it to the front side and create a chamfer.

10 Create a rotating shaft. Cut a ³/₈" (10mm) round bar (rotating shaft) to a length of about 1½" (38mm). Insert it into the hole drilled in step 8 and secure it in place.

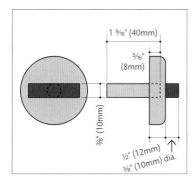

Knob assembly drawing

11 Finish. Clear coat everything except the rotating shaft.

Make the Faucet

12 Shape the faucet body. The tip of the faucet body should have a rounded shape with a radius of approximately ⁹/₁₆" (15mm). Round off any sharp edges and corners with a radius of about ³/₁₆" (5mm).

13 Drill the holes. At the base of the faucet body, locate the center position at a distance of ¹¹/₁₆" (18mm) and drill a hole with a diameter of ³/₈" (10mm) and a depth of ⁵/₁₆" (8mm). Additionally, create a ¹/₁₆" (2mm) through-hole at the center of the previously drilled hole.

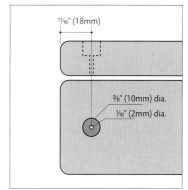

This hole is filled with a dowel after it is screwed to the faucet base.

14 Cut the faucet tip and stem. The faucet tip should measure between ¾" (20mm) and 2⅜" (60mm) in length. From a 1³/₁₆" (30mm) round bar, cut a faucet stem approximately 1"(25mm) long diagonally,at a 25-degree angle on one side.

15 Flatten the two cut-out parts. Drill a ⅜" (10mm) hole in the center of each cutout. For the faucet stem, drill a hole with a depth of ⁹/₁₆" (15mm), and for the faucet tip, drill a hole with a depth of ⁹/₃₂" (7mm). Additionally, create a ⅛" (2mm) through-hole at the center of the faucet tip.

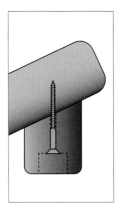

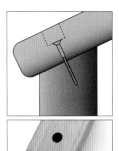

Attach the tip of the faucet by inserting a wood screw through the prepared screw hole created in step 13.

For the faucet stem, secure it by screwing a wood screw into the hole drilled in step 12. To cover the hole, use a ⅜" (10mm) round bar as a dowel, concealing the screw for a seamless finish.

Tip
When drilling holes on the slanted cut surface, ensure that it faces downward to maintain stability. Use a vise or similar tool to hold it firmly in place. It's also possible to make the holes before mounting the parts. Opening the hole will result in a shape similar to the one shown in the picture.

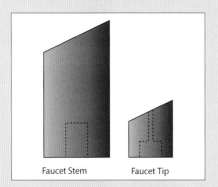

Faucet Stem   Faucet Tip

The hole in the faucet stem is intended for attaching it to the top board of the shelf as a connection point. The through hole at the tip of the faucet is pre-drilled to accommodate a wood screw for assembly purposes.

16 Align the angle of the faucet tip with the faucet stem. Apply glue to the mating surfaces and attach them to the faucet body. Screw the tip of the faucet from the backside and the faucet stem from the front side. Fill any gaps with dowels for a seamless finish.

17 Apply a finish. Apply a finish clear coat to the entire surface of the assembled kitchenette for a smooth and polished appearance.

18 Attach the faucet. Cut a 2" (50mm) length from the bottom end of the faucet stem. Insert the protruding ⅜" (10mm) round bar into the corresponding hole and secure it with adhesive. If the fit is too tight, lightly tap the tip of the round bar with a hammer to adjust it. Take care not to apply excessive force and risk damaging the components.

After assembling the main body, insert it into the hole in the top piece and attach it.

Make the Faucet Handle

19 Drill into the faucet handle. On one side of the faucet handle, drill a hole with a diameter of approximately ¾" (20mm), making it about ⁵/₁₆" (8mm) deep.

20 **Round the corners.** Use a radius of about ⁵⁄₁₆" (8mm) to round the corners of the entire faucet handle, ensuring they are rounded smoothly and accurately.

21 **Cut the stems and shafts.** Cut a 1½" (38mm)-long hanger from a ¾" (20mm) round bar. From a ⅜" (10mm) round bar, cut two stems with lengths that meet the required specifications. Also, cut out two rotating shafts, each measuring 2" (50mm).

22 **Place the handle stem.** Center the handle stem on one end and drill a hole with a diameter of ⅜" (10mm) and a depth of approximately ⁹⁄₁₆" (15mm).

23 **Attach the handle.** Insert the handle stem into the hole drilled in the handle (the end without a hole) and apply glue to secure it. Additionally, insert and glue the rotation axis into the handle stem.

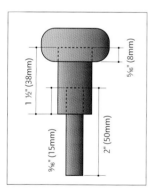

Assembly drawing of the faucet handle.

24 **Apply a finish.** Paint everything except the rotating shaft with a clear coat finish.

After assembling the main body, insert the faucet and handle into their respective holes, and secure them from the backside using a stopper or similar fastening mechanism. This will ensure that the faucet and handle remain in place and properly attached to the kitchenette.

Preparing for Assembly

25 **Prepare the top, sides, and bottom.** For the top board side boards, and bottom board align the back blank approximately ⁹⁄₃₂" (7mm) from the edge on the backside. Carve a groove using a straight bit that is ¼" (6mm) wide and ³⁄₁₆" (5mm) deep. This groove will allow for the insertion and secure placement of the back blank within the main body of the kitchenette.

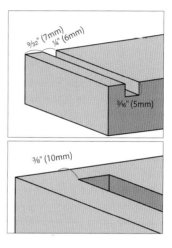

The grooves on the side boards should be carved from end to end on the top side. Leave approximately ⅜" (10mm) of space on both ends of the top and bottom boards to accommodate the grooves. This will ensure proper alignment and fitting of the side boards with the top and bottom parts of the kitchenette.

26 **Attach the sides.** Attach the side panels using a ¼" (6mm) wide straight bit, creating grooves or trenches with a depth of ⅜" (10mm) for seating the components securely.

Carve a horizontal groove approximately 9¹⁄₁₆" (230mm) in length, positioned 9¹⁄₁₆" (230mm) from the bottom edge and ¹⁄₃₂" (1mm) from the back edge.

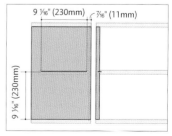

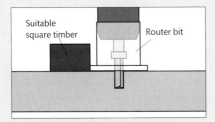
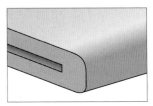

Carve grooves on the left and right ends, and round the front corners. It's important to note that filing the corners becomes challenging after the assembly, so exercise caution during his step.

28 **Drill a hole for the stove knob.** Drill a hole that is 3/8" in diameter (10mm) for the stove knob on the front panel. The hole should be positioned 1 3/16" (30mm) from the top and 3/8" (10mm) from the right edge, with a distance of 10 1/4" (260mm) between the two holes.

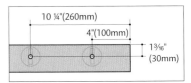

10 1/4"(260mm)

4"(100mm)

1 3/16" (30mm)

The position of the hole where the knob of the stove is attached.

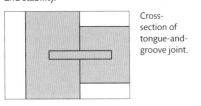
Assembly

29 **Assemble and glue parts together.** Assemble the bottom board side board, back board, shelf board, top board, and front board by referring to the assembly drawing. Glue them together. The back blank should already be prepared. Fit it into the groove. The actual size of the shelf board is 7/32" (5.5mm) thick plywood with the same length as the groove Cut to 9 1/16" (230mm) in length and 3/4" (20mm) in width.

27 **Round the shelf corners.** Round the corners on the front side of the shelf board and create tongue and groove joints on the ends for assembly. Use a router to cut a trench that is 1/4" (6mm) wide and 3/8" (10mm) deep.

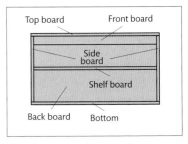

Top board

Front board

Side board

Shelf board

Back board

Bottom

When the back board is put on, the pieces naturally join at right angles.

Tip

Use large F-clamps to tighten both vertically and horizontally until the adhesive cures. If you tighten it unevenly, the adhesive surface may float, so use as many clamps as possible and apply force evenly to the entire board.

30 Glue the knob in place. After the adhesive has fully cured, proceed to glue the stove knob into place. Refer to the drawing (page 177) for the exact location.

Tip

Since it is attached only with adhesive, clamp it firmly until the glue fully cures.

31 Sand and finish. File or sand all corners and hard edges, then apply a clear coat finish

Tip

To achieve optimal results, wrap sandpaper around a long sanding block or piece of scrap wood. This technique will facilitate the process of flattening the surface and rounding the corners. It is crucial to avoid using a small paper file, as it may result in unevenness. Additionally, employing an electric sander can greatly assist in achieving the desired outcome.

32 Prepare pilot holes for screws. Drill pilot holes with a diameter of $1/4$" (6mm) and a depth of $1/8$" (3mm) in five locations on each long leg, and in three locations on each short leg. Additionally, create a $1/16$" (2mm) through-hole in the center.

33 Attach the legs according to the drawing. Following the assembly drawing, apply glue to the back side of the bottom board and attach the legs using screws.

34 Create stoppers. Prepare five stoppers using a $1^{3}/16$" (30mm) round bar, each measuring $3/4$" (20mm) in length. Drill a $3/8$" (10mm) hole in the center of one end to a depth of $9/16$" (15mm)

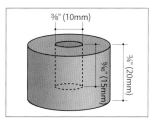

A drawing of the stopper. Make five total—three for the faucet and two for the stove top.

35 Align and secure the faucet. Align the rotation axis of the faucet and faucet handle, then insert them into the holes and secure them with the backside stoppers using adhesive.

Tip

To ensure a proper fit, if the rotating shaft is too tight when inserting it into the top piece, you can file the shaft slightly to make it thinner. However, be cautious not to file too much as it's advisable not to let the tap run idle for extended periods. Use the feel of a real faucet as a reference and exercise care not to remove too much material.

36 Attach the stove knob. Insert the stove knob into the hole in the front board and secure it from the back side using the stopper.

37 Install the tub and adhesive. Place the tub into the cutout on the top board and attach it to the metal. Use a universal adhesive that is compatible with varied components. Ensure good ventilation and allow it to dry completely.

38 Finalize the assembly. Verify the movement of each part to ensure proper assembly and completion.

Kugelbahn

Kugelbahn, meaning "rolling ball" in German, is a toy that features a rotating disk that brings the ball back to the starting point. This intelligent toy is perfect for your study room.

Move

Repeat

▶ Drawing/Pattern: pages 178–181

TOOLS & SUPPLIES

- Drill with 5/64", ¼", ⅜", 1", and 1 ³/₁₆" (2, 6, 10, 25, and 30mm, respectively) bits
- Circular chisel
- Sharp pin vise
- Router with ½" (12mm) bit
- *U*-groove bit
- Saw
- Scroll saw/coping saw
- Back saw/pull saw
- Adhesive
- Hammer
- Sandpaper

▶ **Design and Production: Masahiro Yano (Ken Rack System)**

If you spin the roulette to the right, the ball will enter the hole and go up.

After exiting the hole, the ball will return to the rail.

The ball continues its journey, passing through a tunnel along the way.

CRAFT WITH CARE FOR BALANCE

Take care and ensure the balance of each part as you construct the Kugelbahn. The satisfaction of seeing it roll smoothly is truly rewarding. The ball follows a looped path, descending through the rails carved into the board and returning to the top through the roulette hole. You can use a ¾" (20mm) wooden ball, which is available at craft stores and home centers. If you don't have one, marbles can also be used. The rail grooves can be created using a circular chisel, but for efficiency, a router with a U-groove bit is recommended. This simple toy doesn't require any special materials, but it's important to ensure good balance for each part. If the balance is off, the ball may not roll smoothly or might jump out of the rails, so pay attention to detail while constructing it. It's a good idea to test each part's functionality and make fine adjustments during the process. Making it roll smoothly might be a bit challenging, but the sense of accomplishment when the ball rolls perfectly is worth it. Also, keep in mind that you'll need 1" (25mm) and ¹³⁄₁₆" (30mm) drill bits, specifically "counterbore bits." They are more affordable options and will work well for this project.

Materials Used

For the rails and base, use a plank that is 1" (25mm) thick, and for the roulette, go with a plank that is ¾" (20mm) thick. I recommend using laminated pine lumber or laminated cedar lumber. As for the rotary shaft and handle, use ⅜" (10mm) round bars. Don't forget to include a spacer behind the roulette to adjust the gap using screws. For the part that opens the gap, go for a ¹³⁄₁₆" (30mm) round bar. Cut the board to a thickness of ³⁄₁₆" (5mm) and shape it accordingly. Even if you use a ³⁄₁₆"-thick board and shape it to the desired form, it will work just fine.

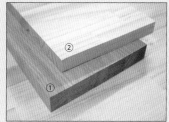

1. **Rail:** 1" (25mm) thick board
2. **Roulette:** ¾" (20mm) thick board
3. **Roulette shaft/handle:** ⅜" (10mm) round bar
4. **Ball:** ¾" (20mm) wooden ball
5. **Spacer:** 1³⁄₁₆" (30mm) round bar or ³⁄₁₆" (5mm) thick board
6. **Wood screws** head diameter ³⁄₁₆" (5mm), length 1 ³⁄₁₆" (30mm); about 13 screws

*Not all materials.

Make a Rail

1 Cut the rails. Cut out rails A to E according to the drawing (page 178).

Tip

When working on the project, the orientation of the wood fibers, whether horizontal or vertical, doesn't have a significant impact. However, if you plan to carve the rail groove by hand using a chisel or similar tools, it is generally easier to cut the rail in the horizontal direction. This allows for smoother and more controlled cuts. It's important to strive for accuracy and precision, especially when creating straight lines and surfaces, particularly the bottom surface where the rail joins the base. While electric tools like circular saws are highly recommended for clean and efficient cuts, you can also achieve good results using a "dozuki saw,"(also known as a Japanese back saw) which excels in making straight cuts. After cutting, it's advisable to trim any rough edges with a planer or similar tools to achieve a clean and polished finish.

2 Drill into rails B and C. Drill 1" (25mm) holes in rails B and C at the specified locations as shown in the drawing.

Tip

When drilling the holes, pay attention to the height difference of ⅛" (3mm). Ensure that you drill the holes in the correct position to ensure smooth rolling of the ball through the tunnel. The height difference is intentional and adds an interesting element to the design.

3 Drill a hole in rail C. Drill a ⅜" (10mm) deep hole in rail C and insert a ⅜" (10mm) hole insert for added functionality.

4 Carve the rail tops. Carve the tops of all the rails diagonally according to the provided drawing to create a distinct shape and enhance the design.

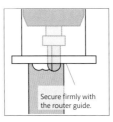

Secure firmly with the router guide.

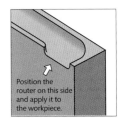

Position the router on this side and apply it to the workpiece.

Run the U-groove bit with a width of approximately ½" (12mm) over the surface about three times, removing any remaining protrusions to achieve a smooth and clean finish.

When reaching the curved section of the rail, approach it from the side with the router bit to carve it smoothly. For refining the fine details, use a circular chisel to trim and shape as needed.

5 Chamfer all rail corners. Carefully chamfer all corners of the rails, except for the bottom that will be in contact with the base. Pay close attention not to round the inside of the rail groove while chamfering.

Tip

When carving the rail, use the actual dimensions provided by the patterns in the book, such as an ¹¹⁄₁₆" (18mm) width and ³⁄₁₆" (5mm) depth. Draw the frame line of the rail using the paper pattern and carefully remove the middle area. Flatten the inside of the rail using a thin round bar wrapped with sandpaper. Pay attention to not rounding the corners of the rail groove to prevent the ball from going off track.

Make a Roulette

6 Draw the roulette. Trace the pattern of the roulette wheel onto your selected board (see illustration on page 107).

Kugelbahn

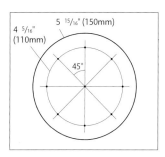

To determine the drilling positions, start by drawing concentric circles of 5 ⅞" and 4 ⁵⁄₁₆" (about 150 and 110mm) 5 ⅞" and 4 ⁵⁄₁₆" (about 150 and 110mm). Then, draw straight lines passing through the center points with a 45-degree shift. Cut along the outer circle, and the intersection point where the inner circle and the straight line meet indicates the drilling position.

7 Cut a circle. Cut out a 5 ¹⁵⁄₁₆" (150mm) circle.

Tip

This circle doesn't need to be perfectly precise but try to clean it up as much as possible for a polished appearance.

8 Drill hole for shaft. Drill a ⅜" (10mm) hole through the center of the circle to insert the rotating shaft.

9 Drill hole in intersection. At the eight points where the inner circle intersects with the straight lines, drill 1³⁄₁₆" (30mm) holes from the back.

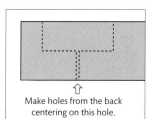

Make holes from the back centering on this hole.

First, drill a 1" (25mm) hole on the front side to a depth of about half the thickness of the wood. Then, using a drill or pin vise, create a small hole through the center. Finally, use a 1 ³⁄₁₆" (30mm) drill bit from the back side to make a hole.

Tip

The purpose of the small hole on the front is to allow the ball to enter and roll to the larger hole on the back without popping out during rotation. To ensure alignment between the front and back holes, you can use a drill or counterbore bit to create a hole just before it fully penetrates. This will result in a small hole at the center, which can serve as a reference point for alignment.

10 Drill a hole for the handle. Drill a ⅜" (10mm) hole for the handle, approximately 1 ⁹⁄₁₆" (about 40mm) away from the center. Stop drilling at a depth of about ⅜" without penetrating through.

11 Add bevels and chamfers. Bevel the outer edges and lightly chamfer the inner edges of the ball hole.

12 Insert the handle piece. Insert a ⅜" (10mm) dowel into the previously drilled hole to serve as the handle, leaving about ¾" (20mm) of the bar protruding.

13 Finish. Apply a finish coat of your choice.

Tip

If you find it difficult to insert the dowel, you can lightly chamfer the tip or gently tap it with a hammer to facilitate insertion. Applying a small amount of wood glue to the tip can also help secure it in place.

14 **Cut out the base.** Cut out the base and chamfer it. Also drill pilot holes for the screws.

Tip

The pilot hole for the screw should be about ¼" (6mm) and have a depth of about ³⁄₁₆" (5mm).

15 **Align the rails.** Align the bottom edges of rails A to D as shown in the drawing (page 178). Position the cage and apply glue to secure it in place. Rail E will be mounted at a later stage.

Tip

For a more secure assembly, it is recommended to follow a specific order when gluing the rails. Start by applying glue to rails B and C, attaching them to the designated positions. Then, proceed to glue rail A, followed by rail D. It is advisable to clamp multiple areas to ensure a strong and tight bond, as gluing on the surface may cause the pieces to shift.

16 **Glue the rails.** Apply glue to the bundled rails A to D and attach them securely to the base. To further reinforce the connection, use screws to tighten the rails from the side. This will ensure a strong and stable assembly.

Tip

Refer to the provided drawing for the exact location. If you have any concerns about the pilot hole of the screw, you can fill it with a dowel of the same diameter. This will provide additional support and ensure a secure attachment.

17 **Cut a spacer from round bar.** Cut a ³⁄₁₆" (5mm)-wide round piece from a 1³⁄₁₆ (30mm) round bar or cut a ³⁄₁₆"-thick board into the desired size. Then, create a ³⁄₈" (10mm) hole in the center to make a spacer.

18 **Insert rotating shaft in rail.** Insert a ³⁄₈" (10mm) dowel into the hole in rail C for the rotating shaft, allowing it to protrude by 1" (25mm). Cut off any excess length.

19 **Add the spacer and roulette.** Thread the spacer and roulette onto the rotating shaft.

Tip

If the roulette wheel is too tight and does not spin, fine-tune it by cutting the spinneret a little. If you shave too much, it will become hollow, so stop when you feel a little resistance.

20 **Tighten rail E.** Tighten rail E with screws. Do this from the back and make sure it's firmly in place.

Tip

Rail E is fixed with only screws without gluing so that the roulette can be removed.

21 **Test ball roll.** Test the ball roll and make adjustments for smooth movement.

22 **Apply a finish.** Remove rail E and roulette, then apply finishing clear coat to complete the assembly.

About Fine Adjustments

For fine adjustments, carefully scrape off areas that hinder smooth ball movement before applying the finishing paint. When the ball stops in the rail or roulette tunnel, diagonally scrape the inside of the hole (in a downward direction) to facilitate better rolling. However, be cautious not to cut too much from the side where the ball exits, as it may become lower than the rail and cause entanglement. Identify any protrusions or irregularities that cause snagging and aim to smoothen those areas. It's important to shave off small amounts at a time while monitoring the situation, as excessive shaving can increase the risk of the ball going off course. If the ball consistently goes off course at the corner of the rail, consider shaving the inner corner slightly. As a last resort, you can attach wood or use wood putty to prevent the ball from escaping.

Kitchenette (Ken Rack System)

Kugelbahn (Ken Rack System)

Swimming Fish

By rotating the handle that links the gear and the piston, you can witness the mesmerizing movement of a wooden fish swimming as if it were alive. This toy holds a captivating allure that enchants children and adults alike.

Move   Repeat

▶ Drawing/Pattern: pages 167–169

TOOLS & SUPPLIES

- Saw
- Scroll saw/coping saw
- Drill and ⅛" (3mm), ³⁄₁₆" (5mm), ⅜" (10mm), and ⁷⁄₁₆" (11mm) bits
- Drum sander
- Sandpaper and file
- Drill press (optional)
- Square
- Clamps
- Adhesive

▶ Design and Production: Toshiyuki Okada
(Woodworking Furniture Studio Mukuri)

CLINK!

Turning a large gear with a handle causes the device to rotate.

TWIST AND TURN!

The device transmits movement to the fish, and it swims beautifully.

CRAFT WITH CARE, AND WATCH THE FISH SWIM!
NO SPECIAL TECHNIQUES REQUIRED.

In simple terms, this toy is a fish swimming that comes to life when you turn the handle. The gears and pistons work together to create a smooth swimming motion for the wooden fish. Despite its simplicity, there is an enchanting charm in its appearance that captivates both children and adults. The fish's body is crafted by cutting it into five parts and joining them using dowels to create flexible joints. The realistic movement of the fish is surprisingly fascinating, making the process of creating just a fish an enjoyable experience. Take your time to carefully fine-tune each part to ensure smooth motion. For the gears and base, it is recommended to use co-core plywood, which is a type of plywood that features a single material for both the core and the surface. Co-core plywood offers a sharp and precise finish. In Japan, the term "veneer" is used interchangeably with plywood.

Materials Used

The fish is made from a board (solid wood) with a thickness of 9/16" (15mm). A 3/16" (5mm) dowel is inserted. All mechanical parts are made of plywood with a thickness of 3/8" to 1/2" (10 to 12mm). It is best to use a material that is as dense as possible and that has little distortion.

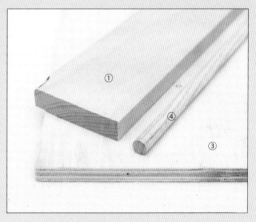

1. **Fish:** 9/16" x 6 1/2" x 6 1/2" (15 x 165 x 165mm)
2. **Fish joint:** 3/16" (5mm) dowel or edge material
3. **Mechanism:** 1/2" (12mm) thick co-core plywood (veneer)
4. **Shaft/dowel:** 3/8" (10mm) round bar

*Not all materials.

Structure and Mechanism of "Swimming Fish"

The structure and mechanism of the "Swimming Fish" toy involves assembling each part separately and connecting them with ⅜" (10mm) dowels. It is important to become familiar with the overall structure and movement of the toy to ensure smooth and flawless operation. By understanding how the components work together, you can fine-tune the toy for optimal performance and address any issues or defects that may arise. This understanding of the mechanism can also serve as a foundation for creating other toys that utilize similar mechanisms, such as gears, expanding your scope of woodworking projects.

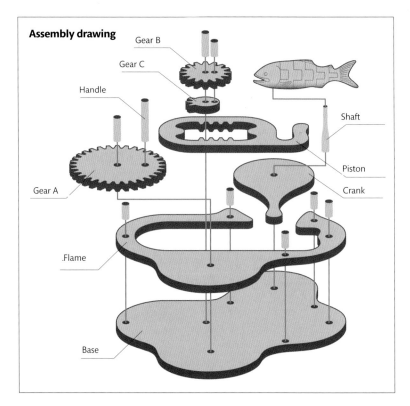

Assembly drawing

Gear B

Gear C

Handle

Gear A

.Flame

Base

Shaft

Piston

Crank

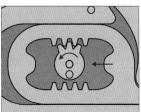

Gears B and C are interlocked and gear C pushes the projection of the piston to move it.

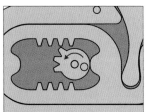

When the piston reaches the end, the teeth and the protrusions are disengaged so it stops easily.

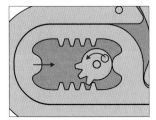

Gear C pushes the protrusion on the opposite side.

Make a Gear

1 **Adhere the gear pattern.** Make a copy of the provided gear pattern and adhere it to your wood.

> **Tip**
>
> The "Swimming Fish" pattern on pages 168-169 of this book is reduced to 50%, so please enlarge it to 200% when copying.

2 **Roughly cut out the gear shape.** Leave some extra material outside the marked line. Then, use a file or sandpaper to make it circular and align it with the outer circle of the gear teeth.

> **Tip**
>
> The circle doesn't affect the movement much unless there is a significant error. If you want a clean finish, use a tool called a drum sander.

After roughly cutting the gear shape out, create a hole of appropriate size in the center and insert a temporary shaft (thick wire, etc.).

Secure the temporary shaft inserted into the appropriate piece and fix it along with the piece to the work board of the drum sander.

Rotate the gear while hitting its side against the drum sander. This process will help achieve a smooth and round shape.

3 **Drill the teeth.** Drill a ⅛" (3mm) hole in the valley of each tooth (the lowest point of the tooth as pictured here).

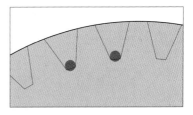

Drill a ⅛" (3mm) hole at the position indicated by the black circle. The exact alignment of the hole with the tooth bottom is not critical for the movement, so a slight misalignment is acceptable.

> **Tip**
>
> By setting the gear assembly under a drilling machine and securing it to a suitable board with a temporary shaft, you can rotate the gear and make holes at equal distances from the center. This method ensures consistent hole placement. Alternatively, you can cut out all the contours using a scroll saw without the need for drilling. Both methods are effective for creating the desired shape and functionality.
>
>
>
> If you have a drill press, it is easy to evenly align the tooth shape.

4 **Create holes for the faucet and handles.** The holes should be roughly ⅜" (10mm) in diameter. Arrange them so they are symmetrical and centered over the sink as pictured.

Cut in a straight line toward the drilled hole.

5 **Shape the teeth.** Adjust the shape of the teeth one by one with a file or sandpaper. Lightly round off the hard corners.

To facilitate sanding, securely attach the gear to a suitable board using a temporary shaft. Fix the board, along with the gear, to the workbench for stability and ease of sanding.

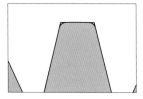

When shaping the gear, be cautious not to over-round the corners. It's important to maintain some sharpness for future adjustments. Lightly rounding the corners will suffice to achieve the desired shape without compromising flexibility.

6 **Check the gears.** After cutting out and shaping all the gears, insert a temporary shaft into the center of each gear. This will allow you to assess how well the gears rotate together. Check if they rotate smoothly and without any obstructions or misalignments. Adjusting at this stage will ensure proper functioning of the mechanism and is much easier than adjusting later.

If you notice any areas where the gears are likely to get caught or encounter friction, use a file or sandpaper to make necessary adjustments.

Tip

Gears may be hollowed out to reduce weight. Please note that if the thickness is too thin, the durability will decrease.

Make the Stove

7 **Cut out the other mechanical parts.** Using a scroll saw, cut out the remaining machine parts, excluding the gears, following the template. Take your time to accurately cut along the designated lines and curves.

Tip

Make copies of the template or pattern for the machine parts. If the pattern is too large to fit on a single piece of paper, you can print it off on multiple sheets and join them together before applying it to your board.

Make a Fish

8 **Apply the pattern.** Affix the fish design onto a $^9/_{16}$" (15mm) thick board using adhesive.

9 **Draw a line.** Extend the hole opening position perpendicular to the board's edge. Draw a vertical line to divide the edge into two equal parts.

Use a square to extend the line from the hole opening position to the edge of the bottom surface. You can use a white paper or a pen to make the line clearly visible.

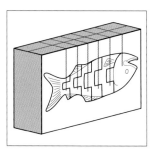

Draw a center line vertically. The points where they intersect are the positions where the drills meet.

10 Drill a hole. Secure the workpiece in a vise to ensure that the drilling position line is vertical. Use clamps or other means to firmly hold it in place. Then, drill a ³/₁₆" (5mm) hole at the intersection of the line drawn in step 9 and the drilling position line.

To ensure the drilling position line is vertical, align the square with the line and securely fix it in place. This will help maintain the vertical orientation while drilling the hole at the intersection of the line drawn in step 9.

Tip

If the hole reaches the joint part, there is no need to penetrate it.

This is the depth of the hole.

These holes are where you will later insert your dowels.

11 Roughly cut out the outline of the fish. Fine shaping will be done later.

Fine molding will be done later, so just the outline is OK here.

12 Cut out the joint. Cut off the joint part with a coping saw or the like.

Check that the holes are not misaligned inside.

13 Adjust the fish's shape. Temporarily insert a ³/₁₆" (5mm) dowel into the drilled hole and secure it in place. This will help stabilize the fish during the adjustment process. With the dowel in place, carefully shape and refine the surface of the fish to achieve the desired appearance.

Insert a rod into the hole and fix the joint. It's a good idea to shave it off a bit to make it thinner so that it can be easily removed later.

Use a chisel or knife to three-dimensionally carve the fish. Pay attention to the contours and textures of the fish, adding depth and shaping the features. Once the carving is complete, use a well-sharpened knife to clean and refine the surface, ensuring a smooth and polished appearance. Take your time and work carefully to achieve the desired result.

Tip

If you're not comfortable with intricate carving, you can still achieve a pleasing result by adding roundness to the fish shape using a knife or file. Focus on creating smooth curves and defining the general form of the fish. To enhance its appearance, draw in the gills and eyes to give it a lifelike quality. If you desire more expression, you can refer to a completed photo of a fish or even observe an actual fish for inspiration. Use these references to guide you in adding details and finishing touches to capture the desired aesthetic.

14 **Round the corners.** Carefully scrape off the sharp corners and edges to make them rounded. This will soften the overall shape and make it more visually appealing. Once the rounding is complete, remove the temporary fastening rod that was used for assembly. Then, attach the joint part securely to the fish. Ensure that the joint is aligned properly and securely fastened to maintain the integrity of the overall structure.

Tip

To achieve a natural look, carefully round the corners of the specific part shown in the picture. However, it's important to avoid making the joint overly rounded, as this can cause excessive bending and make the fish appear unnatural. Connect the joints periodically and carefully shave the corners while checking the degree of bending. This will help you achieve a balanced and visually pleasing result. Remember to take your time and make gradual adjustments to ensure the best outcome.

Just slightly round the corners that hit when bent.

15 **Connect the joints.** To connect the joints, use a ³⁄₁₆" (5mm) dowel and apply a small amount of wood glue along the edge. Be cautious when applying the glue, as it can make the joints difficult to remove if needed in the future. The glue will help provide additional stability and strength to the connections, ensuring that the fish remains securely assembled. Use a modest amount of glue to avoid excessive mess and allow for any potential adjustments or disassembly if required later on.

Tip

Compress the wood by squeezing the dowel and fully insert it into the joint. This will allow the wood to gradually regain its original thickness and create a secure and firm connection.

Roll the dowel while using a wooden block to apply pressure, temporarily thinning it for better fit.

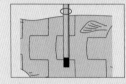

Apply a small amount of adhesive to the end (red circle) before fully inserting the stick to ensure a strong bond.

Complete the fish by cutting the inserted stick at the base and making any necessary adjustments.

Assembly

16 **Cut and insert the shaft.** Cut a ³⁄₈" (10mm) dowel to approximately 5¹⁄₈" (130mm) in length. Insert the cut end into the fish's head. Cut 1³⁄₁₆" (30mm) from the other end to create a ³⁄₁₆" (5mm) shaft.

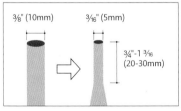

Scrape off the tip of the rod to make it ³⁄₁₆" (5mm) so it can be inserted into the fish's head.

Make sure the rod is thick enough so that when the tip of the rod is inserted into the front hole, it will not spin freely.

17 **Assemble the parts.** Verify the positions of the fixing hole (³⁄₈" [10mm]) and idling hole (⁷⁄₁₆" [11mm]) according to the assembly diagram on page 114.

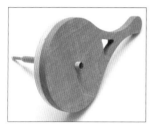

Secure the shaft in the hole of the crank while allowing the hole in the base to rotate freely. It is important to fix the shaft and crank properly to ensure the movement is transmitted to the fish. Pay attention to this step to ensure proper functionality.

Tip

Drill dowel holes only in the frame at first align the positions, and then drill through to the base to avoid misalignment. If dowels can secure the position, glue is not necessary. However, if there is distortion in the base or frame, it can affect movement. Apply glue and use clamps to secure it firmly, if needed. Hold it in place and keep it flat until the glue hardens for optimal results.

18 **Smooth the sides.** Smooth the sides by filing or sanding to eliminate any visible material between the base and frame.

19 **Finish.** Finish the assembly by fine-tuning the movement for smooth operation and applying your preferred paint or finish to achieve the desired look.

Coordination Movements and Finishing

If any gears are hitting or getting caught, identify the problematic area and gradually grind it down for proper clearance. If there is friction causing wood to not slide smoothly, applying a thin layer of wax can improve the movement. For added visual appeal, consider cutting out decorative gears or adding an underwater-themed plaque to the crank. Let your creativity shine through in the finishing touches.

1. Since the gear and piston may rub against each other—causing friction and hindering smooth movement—there are a few approaches to reduce this issue. One method is to insert a piece of thick paper under the piston, elevating it slightly to minimize contact. Alternatively, you can use sandpaper to shave the piston, making it slightly thinner and allowing for smoother operation.

2. For the handle, crafting it from a thick round bar provides a better grip and facilitates easier turning. This enhances the overall usability and performance of the toy.

3. A board with a pattern reminiscent of water is sandwiched between the cranks to create a sense of realism as the fish swim.

Putting Pieces Together

By acquiring the skills to create mechanical parts like gears, you open up a world of possibilities for adding more features to your creations. With careful planning of the gear placement, you have the freedom to explore various configurations. For instance, you can experiment with incorporating multiple fish, or even synchronize their movements using gears. This allows you to unleash your creativity and develop new mechanisms according to your preferences. The potential is limitless, and it all depends on your ideas and imagination. Enjoy the process of exploring and crafting your ideal devices.

Robot Walker Wagon

Put Away   Move

Using one-by material makes the construction process of this wooden robot toy quite straightforward. The key aspect to focus on is the joint part, which I will explain in detail. The majority of the components are made from one-by material, which simplifies the cutting process since it is designed to be flat and doesn't require complex shaping.

▶ Drawing/Pattern: pages 170-174

TOOLS & SUPPLIES

- Drill, with ⅟₃₂"(1mm), ⁵⁄₁₆" (8mm), ⅜" (9mm), ¾" (20mm), and bits
- Saw
- Chisel
- Compass
- Scroll saw/coping saw
- Dovetail saw
- Hammer
- Sandpaper
- Vise

▶ **Design and Production: Tetsuji Takada (Wood Workshop Yamameya)**

FLUTTERING

LISTEN

The expression can be arranged as you like. It is okay to attach decorations such as antennas.

The robot's legs flap with a stick attached to the axle of the front wheel.

The robot's arms have unique movements that match the rotation of the rear wheels.

EASY TO MAKE WITH ONE-BY LUMBER

The highlight of the construction lies in the joint part of the arm, which enables smooth and clean bending. To achieve a flawless outcome, intermittent processing techniques are employed. One such technique is the use of a tool called a dovetail saw, which plays an active role in shaping the joint part precisely.

When the rear wheels rotate, the robot's arm exhibits unique movements that add an element of intrigue to the toy. This interaction between the rotation of the wheels and the arm's motion enhances the overall play experience.

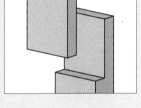

"Ai-kiri" (a Japanese term that roughly translates to "cutting with love") is a technique that involves cutting off half of the thickness of the material in an alternating pattern. When executed meticulously, this method results in perfectly connected cut edges, giving the appearance of a seamless single piece of wood. It requires precision and attention to detail to achieve a smooth and consistent outcome. This technique can be employed in various woodworking projects to create visually appealing joints and connections.

Materials Used

The materials used for this project include the "carrying platform side board" and "cargo platform crosspiece," which have dimensions of 4¼" (105mm) in width and 1³⁄₁₆" (30mm) in thickness. It is recommended to use studs, but be cautious as some studs may be 4¾" (120mm) wide. Japanese cedar is the chosen material for this project. All components are half the thickness (¾" [19mm]) of a two-by material known as "one-by."

The robot arm, handle arm, and stock part are made from 1" x 1½" (25 x 38mm) material, while the robot legs, robot shoes, and soles are also crafted using the same

material. The board measures 1" x 4" (25 x 100mm), and the robot body is created using 1" x 12" (25 x 305mm) material, which can be easily cut out according to the desired specifications.

The wheels are cut from 1" x 10" (25 x 250mm) material. After cutting them into 4⁵⁄₁₆" (110mm) squares, the final shaping is done using a scroll saw. For circles with a diameter of 4⁵⁄₁₆" (110mm), you can either cut them out or search for pre-existing pieces of wood with similar dimensions. Alternatively, you can find a piece of wood with a suitable shape and use it as is.

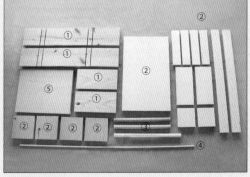

*Not all parts.

1. **Cargo platform** side panel/cargo platform crossbar
2. **Cedar studs** with a width of 4¼" (105mm) (2 pieces)
3. **Robo torso** / Robo arm / Robo leg / Robo shoe /Wheel / Bottom board / Handle arm / Robo leg bearing: One-by material ¾" x 1 ½" (20 x 38mm) used for various components
4. **Handle/axle:** ¾" (20mm) round bar
5. **Joint/cam/robo leg shaft:** ⁵⁄₁₆" (8mm) round bar
6. **Stopper**

HOW
TO MAKE

Clipping

1 Cut out the parts. Cut out each part according to the instructions on the drawing (pages 170–174). For the handle and axle (¾" [20mm] round bar), leave them about ¾" longer than the working dimension for adjustment after installation.

2 Cut the robot body. From the 1 x 12 material, cut the robot body slightly narrower and remove the corners as shown in the drawing. If desired, you can also paint or decorate the face.

3 Cut the wheels. Cut the wheels into squares measuring approximately 4½" x 4½" (115 x 115mm). If using 1 x 10 material, cut it in half. The final shape will be a circle with a diameter of 4⁵⁄₁₆" (110mm), so slight variations are acceptable.

4 Attach the handle arm. Attach the handle arm to the cargo platform. Drill two ⁵⁄₁₆" (8mm) holes on the mounting position where the ¹⁄₁₆" (2mm) hole is located. Also, drill a ⁵⁄₁₆" (8mm) hole where the arm will be attached.

5 Create the stopper. Create the stopper using a board with a thickness of about ⅜" (10mm). Cut it into a circle shape and make a ⁵⁄₁₆" (8mm) hole in the center. Keep it open, and you will need a total of six stoppers, with four measuring 1⁹⁄₁₆" (40mm) and two measuring 1³⁄₁₆" (30mm).

6 Drill holes. On the side board of the cargo platform, drill holes of ¹⁄₃₂" (1mm) and ⁵⁄₁₆" (8mm) at the positions where the robo leg bearing and dowels will be inserted.

7 Prepare handle and axles. Cut three pieces of round bar, two for the axles and one for the handle, to a length of approximately 12¼" (310mm). Cut them to the same length while attaching them together.

Make a Carrier

8 Cut a groove. Using the drawing as a guide, cut a groove on the inner face of the bed side panel to accommodate the crosspiece. Pay attention to the position and width of the groove as indicated in the drawing.

Tip

The assembly method used in this project is called "in-and-out," where the small part is inserted into the groove. Create a groove with a width of 1³⁄₁₆" (30mm) and a depth of ⅜" (10mm), at intervals of several millimeters. Place the wood on the marked area and tap it gently from behind with a hammer to make it fit. Use a chisel to trim and refine the groove for a clean finish.

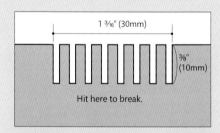

9 After inserting the crosspieces into the groove to create a frame, secure them by inserting dowels from the side. The dowels should go in to a depth of about 1⁹⁄₁₆" (40mm) to ensure a sturdy connection.

Chamfering the corners of the crossbar makes it easier to insert.

Tip

This is the basic procedure for doweling.

Using a ⁵⁄₁₆" (8mm) drill bit, drill a hole into the rung where the dowel will be inserted. The hole should be 1 ⁹⁄₁₆" (40mm) deep.

Insert the round dowel into the pre-drilled hole. If the dowel is too tight to fit, you can chamfer the tip to make it thinner, which will make it easier to insert.

Once the dowel is inserted, cut off any protruding portion at the root using a saw. Be careful not to damage the surrounding wood.

Use a chisel to smooth out the cut surface of the dowel, ensuring a clean and flush finish.

Make a Wheel

10 Draw a circle. Take a board cut to 4¹⁄₂" x 4¹⁄₂" (115 x 115mm) and draw a diagonal line across it. Using a compass with a width of 2³⁄₁₆" (55mm), draw a circle with a diameter of 4⁵⁄₁₆" (110mm), centered at the intersection point of the diagonal line.

11 Draw concentric circles. For the wheels, draw concentric circles with a width of 1³⁄₈" (35mm) centered on the two rear wheels. Additionally, mark one point as the position to hold the handle, ensuring it is aligned with the concentric circles.

Tip

To ensure the strength of the wheel, it is important to position the center point and the fixing position of the handle side by side when the grain direction is turned sideways. This arrangement will provide better structural support and stability for the wheel.

Pay attention to the positional relationship between the center point and the fixing position of the handle. If they are not aligned properly, there is a risk of the dowels cracking when pressure is applied. Ensure that the center point and the handle fixing position are positioned correctly to prevent any potential issues.

---

12 Drill a hole in the circle. Create a ⁵⁄₁₆" (8mm) hole at the center of the circle and at the fixed position of the handle.

13 Cut along the line. Cut along the 4 ⁵⁄₁₆" (110mm) circle line to form the wheel. It will move and make a rattling sound. The wheel does not need to be a perfect circle, as it adds to the toy-like charm.

14 **Insert a dowel into the hole you cut.**
Cut a ⁵/₁₆" (8mm) round bar to a length of
2¼" (57mm) and insert it into the hole drilled
in step 12. The diameter of the hole and the rod
should match, allowing for a snug fit. Secure it
in place. If insertion is difficult, chamfer the
edges of the stick slightly to facilitate insertion.

Tip

If the dowel is too thin and the hole is
loose, you can apply a thin layer of instant
adhesive to the position where it fits into the
hole. Allow it to harden and then smooth
the surface with sandpaper. Alternatively,
you can adjust the thickness little by little
without using adhesive to achieve a snug fit.
Aim for an optimal thickness that provides a
secure hold.

Make Front Wheel Axle

15 **Cut the front wheel axle.** Place the axle
for the front wheels 3 ⁹/₁₆" (90mm) from
both ends of the rod and drill a ⁵/₁₆" (8mm) hole
through the center of the rod at that position.
To allow for movement of the robot leg up and
down, open the two holes at a shifted angle of
approximately 90-degree (the angle can be
determined visually).

Tip

When drilling a hole in a round bar, it is
necessary to use a V-shaped stand or vise to
hold it firmly in place so that it does not roll.
There are also drill stands that make it easier
to drill holes in round bars. You can find
these in home centers or online.

A drill stand that makes
it easier to drill holes in
round bars.

The rod is fixed in the
V-shaped groove and
can be drilled in the
exact center.

Alternatively, take
two triangular pieces
of wood on a board
and make a V-shaped
groove. Use this as
a platform.

Insert an ³/₁₆" (8mm) dowel into the two holes and
check if they are aligned correctly at the desired
90-degree angle. Ensure that the dowel fits securely
and allows smooth movement.

Make Robot Legs

16 Shape the shoes. Arrange the shape of the tip of the robot shoes as you like. It is okay to leave them square.

17 Secure the shoes. Attach dowels to the tip (small end) of the robot leg to secure the robot shoes.

18 Drill bearing holes. Drill an $^{11}/_{32}$" (9mm) hole at the center of the robot leg for bearings.

19 Install bearings. Apply adhesive to the base end of the back of the robot leg. Install the bearing. Determine the position while passing the leg shaft, and make sure both legs are parallel.

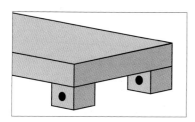

Attach two bearings to the base of the robot legs.

Make a Robot Arm

20 Prepare the robot arms. Divide the four robot arms into two "upper robot arms" and two "lower robot arms." Draw lines on each arm to mark the cutting points.

Use the dovetail saw to draw a line in the center of the arm. This will serve as a guide for cutting.

To avoid mistakenly cutting off the wrong parts, mark the unnecessary sections with a pencil or similar tool.

Tip

Position the cutting edge of the saw about halfway through the thickness of the arm. Align it with the $^3/_8$" (10mm) mark and make sure the center line is aligned as shown in the photo below. Apply gentle pressure and begin the cutting motion. If the reference surface (the main body of the tool) is oriented in one direction, the gap will be completed even if the center line is not perfectly accurate.

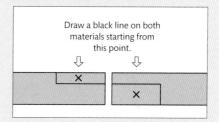

Draw a black line on both materials starting from this point.

It is fine if the thickness is slightly shifted from the center, as long as the two pieces overlap seamlessly when combined.

21 **Put pattern on the wood.** Refer to the drawing and copy the shape and hole positions of the base (shoulder), joint, and tip (hand) to their respective positions on the materials.

22 **Drill the holes.** Drill holes at the designated hole positions for both sides of the robot arms. Take note that the hole on the tip (hand) side of the robot arm is $^{11}/_{32}$" (9mm), while the hole on the root (elbow) side is $^{5}/_{16}$" (8mm). Ensure accuracy to avoid any mistakes.

23 **Cut off the excess.** Use a saw to cut off the unnecessary parts as marked, and then use a chisel to trim and clean up the cut edges.

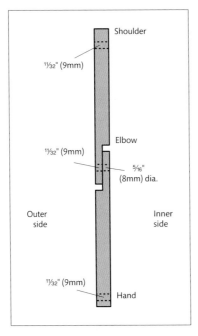

Overall image of the robot arm. Note that the elbow joint is only $^{5}/_{16}$" (8mm) for the hole on the inside.

Tip

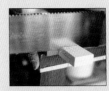

Begin by making a horizontal pull cut from the side of the material. This initial cut will create a guideline for further shaping.

Proceed with a vertical pull cut from the front edge to remove the unnecessary parts. Take care not to make the thickness too thin and ensure you are cutting at the intended locations.

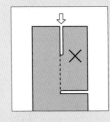

Consider the thickness of the saw blade and adjust your cuts accordingly to maintain the desired thickness of the material. It is important to insert the blade fully to avoid any irregularities.

After the cuts are complete, use a chisel to straighten the edges and align the gaps perfectly. This will help achieve a clean and seamless appearance.

24 **Trim the edges.** Trim the edges of the robot arm along the line drawn in step 21 and adjust the shape as needed. Take care to create a smooth and clean edge. Customize the shape of the hand according to your preference, giving it a unique and desired appearance.

25 **Complete the joints.** For the joints, cut them to a length of 2 ¼"(57mm). Insert the dowel ⁵⁄₁₆" (8mm) into the elbow hole located underneath the robot arm and secure it firmly. Use a 1 ⁹⁄₁₆" (40mm) stopper to fasten the joint elbow, ensuring stability and proper alignment.

Secure the ⁵⁄₁₆" (8mm) rod in the ¹¹⁄₃₂" (8.5mm) hole. This provides flexibility and allows for smooth movement of the joint.

Assemble

26 **Secure the bottom boards.** Place the two bottom boards in a way that covers the bottom of the cargo bed and secure them with dowels. Attach the other board to the back of the robot body, fixing it with a dowel from the side according to the position shown in the drawing.

27 **Put the robot in the arms.** Sandwich the handle and robot body between the two handle arms. Fix the handle in place with glue. Align the lower end of the robot body with the shoulder area and use dowels to appropriately secure the holes in the excess handle trim.

Tip

At this stage, ensure that the dowel is positioned on the outer side of the handle arm. If it protrudes by approximately 1³⁄₁₆" (30mm), trim it. This will allow for the attachment of the robot arm's shoulder.

28 **Attach the handle and body.** Angle the handle arm and robot body at seven degrees from the vertical and attach them to the cargo platform. Secure them in place by inserting dowels. Ensure that both arms are parallel during attachment.

29 **Attach the leg.** Cut the robo leg shaft to a length of 9 ⅞" (250mm) and fix the robo leg by passing it through the robo leg bearing.

30 **Attach the axle and wheel.** Once the axle has been inserted through the axle bearings on the cargo platform, insert the end into the wheel and secure it. Trim the axle to an appropriate length.

Tip

The wheels should be fixed with a slight clearance of ⅛" (3mm) above the cargo platform to prevent rubbing. Ensure proper positioning to avoid interference. Also, note that the positions of the joint rods for the rear wheels are different on the left and right sides. This ensures that the robot arms move alternately and synchronized.

31 **Cut a cam.** Cut a cam with a length of approximately 2¾" (70mm) from a ⁵⁄₁₆" (8mm) round bar and fix the protrusions on both sides to roughly the same length. Insert the cam into the hole drilled in the front wheel axle.

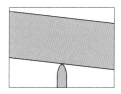

If the tip of the cam is flattened, it moves smoothly.

If the robot legs wobble from side to side, insert an appropriate piece of wood (spacer) between them to fix this.

32 **Affix the arm.** Insert the robot arm into the rod protruding from the shoulder and rear wheel. Fix the outside with a stopper using 1⁹⁄₁₆" (40mm) for shoulder fixation and 1³⁄₁₆" (30mm) for hand fixation.

33 **Refine the joints.** Smooth the joints and wheels of each part. Rotate and confirm that there is no looseness in the fixed parts.

Toy House

Put Away   Move

Create a toy box designed like a charming house where toys can find their home after playtime. Attach a handle that secures the lid using a lanyard-like mechanism with a flag. The key feature is the double locking mechanism, ensuring the lid stays securely closed.

▶ Drawing/Pattern: pages 165-167

TOOLS & SUPPLIES

- Drill with ¹⁄₃₂" and ³⁄₁₆" (1 and 5mm) bits
- Saw
- Scroll saw/coping saw
- Chisel
- Large clamps
- Planer
- Hammer
- Sandpaper and/or file
- Hammer

▶ **Design and Production: Tetsuji Takada**
(Wood Workshop Yamameya)

Take out the flag.

Remove the handle.

Open the lid and put toys into the box.

CREATE USING DOWELING

Assemble a durable toy box using the woodworking technique called doweling. Pay close attention to the way the board parts are put together before starting the construction. If you are not familiar with doweling, it is recommended to practice beforehand. Having a large F-clamp or belt clamp for temporary assembly will be convenient. The natural texture of the wood can be visually appealing even without coloring, but adding a touch of color to certain parts, such as the window frame and handle as shown in the sample photo, can create a visually striking effect. Enjoy the process of transforming the material's color and creating a visually appealing toy box.

Materials Used

For the main parts that make up the house, we use 'one-by' lumber, which is half the thickness of two-by lumber. You can easily make the side panel, bottom panel, and top panel with 1" x 10" material (25 x 256mm), and the front panel and top panel with 1" x 12" (25 x 300mm) One-by material may have slight variations in size, but as long as the lengths are the same, you can proceed without any issues. For the other parts, you have flexibility in choosing the material, but ensure that the "warp stop" is able to withstand any warping in the side blank. It is recommended to choose the hardest material available.

* Not all parts.

1. **Front panel:** One-by material
   Side panel: One-by material
   Bottom panel: One-by material
   Top panel: One-by material
2. **Handle:** ¾" (20mm) round bar
3. **Anti-warp boards :** ¾" x 1" (20 x 25mm) rectangular lumber (preferably hard material)

4. **Window frame:** ¾" (19mm) square lumber
5. **Flag pole/window frame dowel:** 5/32" (5mm) round bar
6. **Body dowel:** 5/16" (8mm) round bar
7. **Flag:** Cloth, paper, soft leather, etc. (optional)

Clipping

1 **Cut the front, side, bottom, and top panels.** Use the dimension drawing as a guide and refer to faces A-C for each figure (pages 165–167).

2 **Cut a window.** Make a round hole (0.21mm) for the handle in the front panel and cut out a window 1³/₁₆" x 2 ³/₄" (30 x 70mm). Refer to drawings A and B for guidance.

> **Tip**
>
> The diameter of the hole for the handle is ¹/₃₂" (1mm) larger than that of the handle so that the rod can be passed through smoothly and the error in the hole position is covered.

3 **Measure and determine the length of the warp prevention pieces.** These pieces are used to prevent warping of the side panel. To calculate the length, measure the height of the side panel and cut the anti-warp board so you will have a ⁷/₈" (23mm) gap on each end.

4 **Cut out the window panes.** Cut out 8 pieces for the window frame, each with a length of 2 ³/₄" (70mm). Additionally, on the upper crossbar (2), make a ³/₈" (10mm) round hole with an edge or ³/₁₆" (5mm) in depth at the center.

> **Tip**
>
> If you are using 1 x 10 material, the length of the anti-warp pieces should be 7 ⁹/₁₆" (192mm). Measure and calculate accordingly based on the dimensions of your specific material.

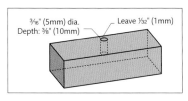

Make a ³/₁₆" (5mm) hole in the center of the top.

5 **Cut out the handle.** Cut the handle from a ³/₄" (20mm) round bar to a length of 9 ¹¹/₁₆" (246mm). Trim the flag poles (³/₁₆" [5mm] round poles) to approximately 4³/₄" (120mm) in length.

6 **Chamfer the corners.** Chamfer all the corners of the parts that do not meet other parts.

Attach The Anti-Warp Material To The Side Blank

7 **Attach a warp stop.** On both sides of the back edge of the side panel, attach a warp stop in the center. Leave a ⁷/₈" (23mm) gap on both ends. Temporarily assemble with a clamp, ensuring that the side panel and the anti-warp are tightly in contact and flattened.

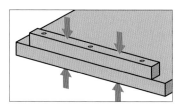

Fix by tightening firmly.

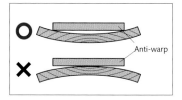

Since the cross-grain board warps toward the front side of the wood, the warp stopper is tightened from the front side of the wood.

Tighten with two clamps.

8 **Insert the dowel.** Insert the dowel coated with wood glue to secure it firmly. Allow the glue to set, then remove the clamp.

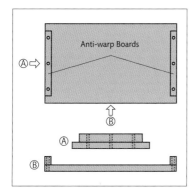
Hammer the dowels in three places to ensure a firm hold.

Make a Flag

9 **Attach cloth to the tip.** Attach a triangular piece of cloth or paper to the tip of the flagpole. Additionally, you can attach a safety ball to prevent injuries, if desired.

You can arrange the shape of the flag as you like.

Body Assembly

10 **Assemble the top and bottom.** Assemble the side panel and top panel as shown below and secure them using a belt clamp or F-clamp. Ensure that the top and bottom are firmly fixed. Position the board so that it slightly overlaps the anti-warp by a few millimeters ($3/32$" [2.5mm] on each side) inward from the edge of the side panel.

11 **Join the bottom and sides.** Attach the bottom panel to the side board by hammering dowels from the side (approximately 3 places on one side as indicated in the diagram). Take care not to secure the top panel as it will be the lid.

Temporarily assemble the side , top, and bottom panels with clamps.

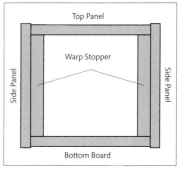
The top and bottom edges of the side panel protrude slightly.

12 **Remove the top panel.** Do so after loosening the clamps.

13 **Temporarily attach the front panel.** Temporarily attach the front panel to both sides of the body using clamps. Ensure that the width of the front panel is slightly wider and that it protrudes evenly from the side panel. Refer to drawings E and F for the assembly process.

14 **Attach the lower end.** Shift the lower end of the front panel ⅜" (10mm) outside the side panel, making the box stand on the front boards on both sides. Once the position is determined, attach it by hammering dowels in 6 places on one side. See Drawing F for the dowel positions.

15 **Remove the clamps.** Remove the clamps once the glue has dried.

16 **Glue the window frame.** Apply glue to the window frame and secure it around the window hole using double bolts. Use a ³⁄₁₆" (5mm) round bar with a depth of approximately 1" (25mm). Additionally, create two holes in the flag as mentioned in step 4 and make sure to use the corresponding rungs for insertion.

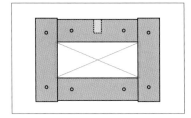

The window frames on both sides are arranged to slightly hide the window holes.

Assembling the Lid

17 **Check the fit.** Check if the top board fits snugly in the main unit. If it is too tight or unfit, use a planer or file to adjust the edges and edges of the top panel.

18 **Align the top panel.** Align the top blank with the main body when it is housed (lid closed) and mark the position. Copy the position of the hole for the round bar onto the front blank.

19 **Attach the top panel.** Attach the top blank by hitting dowels from the back side. Remove the top blank during this process. The mounting position should be ⅛" (3mm) inside the edge of the top blank to prevent rubbing against the front blank of the main unit. Ensure equal protrusion width on the left and right corners.

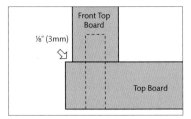

Attach the top board, positioning it ⅛" (3mm) inside from the edge of the top blank.

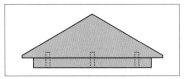

Secure the top board by inserting approximately three dowels from the back side of the top board.

Toy House

20 **Trim the top piece.** Trim about ⅛" (3mm) off each side of the top board to create a ¾" (19mm) protrusion at the left and right corners.

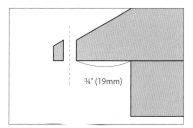

Cut the left and right corners of the top board so that the protruding width is ¾" (19mm).

Tip

Use the top board as a warp stopper and shape it into a triangle, if needed. Place it on a flat surface before cutting. Remove the anti-warp from steps 7 and 8. Tighten firmly to flatten the top board.

Adding the Handle

21 **Secure the front and top.** Align the front panel hole with the top blank and secure them together with the lid closed.

22 **Insert the handle.** Insert the handle round bar into the designated hole and trim it to the length of the window frame.

23 **Drill the holes for the flag.** Mark and drill two holes in the window frame to match the positions for inserting the flag. Ensure they are parallel.

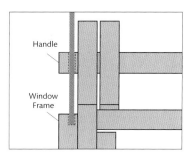

Make a hole in the handle so that the flag stick can be inserted into the gray part. The same goes for the other side.

Tip

When drilling holes for the flag in the window frame, make one hole first and then determine the position of the second hole while inserting the flag. This ensures proper alignment and stability. Remember that the hole in the window frame should be ³/₁₆" (5mm) and the hole in the handle should be ¹¹/₆₄" (4.5mm) to prevent the flag pole from slipping out.

24 **Insert the flag.** Now, you can insert the flag and lock the lid. Ensure everything fits together correctly.

Toy House (Wood Workshop Yamameya)

Robot Walker Wagon (Wood Workshop Yamameya)

Woodwork Kikkoro

Kikkoro's toys are inherently adorable. Their smooth and tactile nature captivates children and makes them an ideal choice as a "first gift" for special occasions. The use of natural paint brings out the natural beauty of the wood, ensuring safety and peace of mind. Kikkoro's toys feature timeless mechanisms that continue to fascinate children, preserving their freshness and charm. The weekends are often filled with nationwide crafting events, where Kikkoro showcases their creations. Mr. and Mrs. Kikkoro personally handle all aspects of production, giving meticulous attention to each piece. Through these events, they have the opportunity to directly observe children's reactions, which fuels their imagination and results in toys that truly resonate with young ones. The simple and gentle designs are not only perfect for children but also appeal to adults seeking the warmth of wood. You can purchase their works from authorized dealers or at exhibition events.

For more information, please visit their homepage (https://kikkoro.jp/).

This animal series features charming characters with tires, including the adventurous "Crocodile." Another popular character in their collection is the whimsical "Ghost" vase. Additionally, the Animal Series offers the graceful "Giraffe" with tires. These unique creations bring joy and imagination to both children and adults alike.

The workshop is located along a peaceful and lush path. It specializes in working with wood, creating not only toys but also furniture and various other items. Each piece is meticulously crafted by Akiko Iwai, who eagerly awaits the reactions of children. Leading the production process is Mr. Kenichi Iwai.

Comomg

This is a captivating and insightful book that celebrates the power of children's imagination. It offers an abundance of joy and amusement through its engaging games and activities. As you hold the book in your hands, you'll feel a comforting and familiar touch, creating a sense of security. Unako Mam's work, led by Kazuto Komatsu, the representative, and a team of dedicated individuals, including Mr. Miyazaki and Mr. Ito, carries on with the same passion and commitment.

Within these pages, you'll discover a safe and inviting space where children can freely play, surrounded by their loved ones, be it their fathers, mothers, or friends. There is a shared passion among all those involved in creating Maamu, fueled by the desire to design new and innovative toys. The process of making these toys becomes an enjoyable form of play itself. We aim to share this experience, fostering a deep appreciation for the significance of play and the role toys play in shaping lasting childhood memories.

Mr. Miyazaki, in particular, recognized the charm of creating toys that leave a lasting impact on children. Additionally, Mr. Ito's first wooden toy was crafted within the walls of Komamu's workshop. It is evident that the joy and anticipation seen in children's faces are at the heart of the toymaking process, adding an extra layer of enchantment to the art of creating.

Learn more at https://comomg.co.jp/.

The studio is always bustling with creators. Works are sold at dealers nationwide and online shops.

Acroge Furniture

Acroge Furniture is a furniture workshop located near Koku Park in Tokorozawa City. We specialize in custom furniture orders and provide maintenance and repair services. Our focus is on showcasing the natural beauty and texture of solid wood. Our pieces are not only functional but also visually pleasing, evoking a sense of awe. Each order is meticulously handcrafted, taking into consideration the customer's preferences and requests. We strive to convey the inherent qualities of wood through careful selection and craftsmanship, ensuring that the grain and character of the wood are maximized. Skilled artisans pay attention to even the smallest details, meticulously finishing every surface, corner, and curve. We deeply understand the subtleties of materials and aim to express their uniqueness. The simplicity of our designs is enhanced by the craftsmanship and dedication of our artisans. Learn more at https://www.acroge-furniture.com/.

Meet Representative Kuniaki Kishi, a visionary dedicated to the concept of his store. Inspired by the arrival of his own child, he pours the same passion into crafting toys as he does with furniture. The result is a stunning combination of organic curves and natural woodgrain. With 10 full-scale woodworking workshops, Kishi imparts his expertise through hands-on classes, empowering students to create their own masterpieces.

Ken Rack System

Ken Rack System Co., Ltd. is a company that specializes in creating wooden equipment and toys for preschools and kindergartens. It is a warm and inviting place where many people can gather and enjoy playing together. Originally, woodworking was a hobby for Mr. Yano, an engineer who had a passion for both woodworking and children. He started by making children's furniture and toys for his own enjoyment.

The commercialization of his creations began with the creation of "cha," which received positive feedback and requests from kindergarten teachers and others. Through thorough discussions and continuous improvement, they strive to provide better products. They understand the importance of children being able to interact with natural materials like wood, and they use their own experiences and expertise to create unique and engaging spaces.

Their dedication and commitment to taking on new challenges serve as the driving force behind their ability to produce innovative and exciting products that are highly appreciated today.

Among their creations is a sand art playground equipment table, which allows children to play with sand and observe it falling through a mechanism. This design encourages repeated play and was developed in collaboration with a principal, earning them recognition and winning a prize in a city competition.

Additionally, they have designed interior doors for nursery schools with child-proof locks at the top to prevent them from being opened by young children. They also offer simple and rounded chairs specifically designed for children.

Through their passion for woodworking and commitment to creating products that are both practical and enjoyable for children, Ken Rack System Co., Ltd. continues to bring cool and fun products to life. Learn more at http://www.kodomonokoe.com/.

The "Sand Art Playground Equipment Table" is a unique playground equipment designed by Mr. Masahiro Yano. It provides a delightful experience of sand art as the entire top board illuminates, creating a visually captivating display. Additionally, it offers the joy of rolling marbles, adding an interactive element to the play.

Woodwork Furniture Workshop Mukuri

Mukuri is a creator who specializes in crafting various playful items such as furniture, accessories, and toys from wood. Toshiyuki Okada, a woodworking artist, infuses his works with a captivating and unique world-view. His masterpiece "Sugar" received the Grand Prize at the Wood Turning Exhibition. This work showcases elegant curves and intricate mechanisms using gears and rotations, blending Mukuri's distinct style and craftsmanship. Despite its artistic appeal, these creations remain functional tools, embodying the fusion of art and utility.

Mukuri's works are exhibited in various locations, particularly in Tokyo, and can also be found online for viewing and purchase. Their collection encompasses a range of items, each showcasing the artist's mysterious charm. Among them, the sugar pot stands out, featuring a handle that, when twisted, opens the lid as the main body rotates, mimicking the movements of a living creature. Accessories with Mukuri's unique gimmicks are also popular, such as the intricately designed "Ring Box" inspired by the organic curves of plants. Explore Mukuri's creations to experience the enchantment they offer.

In the captivating world of Toshiyuki Okada's unique creations, resembling paintings, machine enthusiasts are drawn to the allure of gears, cranks, cams, chains, and other intricate mechanisms. The works featured in this book, including the "Swimming Fish," possess a strong charm that captivates not only children but also adults. You can find a video showcasing these creations on the website. One of my personal favorites is the "Kawasaki Mach III," which showcases Mr. Toshiyuki Okada's mechanical prowess and may even appeal to motorcycle enthusiasts. Additionally, Mr. Okada conducts woodworking classes where he imparts his skills and technique, earning him a well-deserved reputation. Learn more at http://www.mukuri.com/top.html.

Wood Studio Yamameya

Mr. Tetsuji Takada, the talented furniture and interior designer of Yamameya, is known for his authentic craftsmanship and exquisite designs of furniture and miscellaneous goods. His work showcases a skillful expression of solid wood, capturing its texture and beauty. What sets his work apart is the constant presence of fresh ideas and creativity. He combines usability, aesthetic appeal, and the natural curves and quality of wood to create intriguing and interesting pieces that engage the audience.

His creations extend beyond wood, incorporating materials like leather and metal, resulting in a diverse range of products. At exhibitions where he collaborates with family members, he not only presents new designs but also provides comprehensive proposals, considering how his creations can be used in different situations. Every aspect, from materials to shapes and textures, reflects his deep commitment and love for his craft, as well as the serene beauty of nature. The gentleness and kindness embedded in his work resonate with the viewers.

At his workshop located in the tranquil rural area of Kuki City, Saitama Prefecture, various equipment and materials are meticulously arranged. The workshop is a hub of creativity, where Mr. Takada brings his ideas to life. Some of his notable creations include the spoke chair, which showcases the craftsmanship and warmth of wood in its curves and angles, and the child chair that emphasizes the natural texture of wood, using safe paint. From hand-carved stack-type stools to hand-drawn sketches of toys featured in this book, each piece exudes a unique depth and richness of flavor.

Mr. Takada is a versatile designer known for his skillful craftsmanship and diverse range of products. His creations, such as the stick aroma "Korobox" and aged wood photo frames, exude a unique charm that adds character to any space. The rustic wooden sign adorning his studio reflects the natural and organic atmosphere that permeates his designs. Learn more at http://www7a.biglobe.ne.jp/~yamameya/.

Tsugumi Kougeisha Hyakkaten Higurashi Store

"Hyakkaten Higurashi Store" is a charming shop located in Chichibu city, home to Tsugumi Craft House. The store is owned and operated by Mr. and Mrs. Yumiko Adachi, with woodwork artist Shiji Adachi leading the creative endeavors. Mr. Shijima, the owner, is an accomplished painter and sculptor who honed his skills in the United States, specializing in engraving and woodblock printing. His passion for woodworking led to the establishment of Tsugumi Kogeisha, where he currently engages in producing unique artworks using natural materials, including reclaimed wood from old folk houses. The creations emanate an organic beauty and feature a touch of whimsical charm. The meticulous attention to material selection and craftsmanship adds to their undeniable appeal.

Yumiko, along with her dedicated team, runs the gallery shop called "Higurashi Store." The shop not only showcases their own creations but also serves as a platform for various craft exhibitions and workshops, embracing different artistic genres. The space itself is a renovated row house that boasts a rich history of over 80 years. In addition to their artistic displays, the shop offers an array of toys and organic food, creating a delightful atmosphere for visitors to explore and enjoy. Learn more at https://tugumi2009.wixsite.com/tugumicraft.

Tsugumi Craft House offers a delightful collection of wooden toys that exude a warm and inviting feel. These toys showcase the meticulous craftsmanship and attention to detail that make them truly special. The handcrafted nature of the toys creates a unique and charming atmosphere. The tableware, crafted with care, has a distinct feel when held, likely due to the meticulous handiwork involved. Additionally, the cutlery is safe for use as it is finished with natural oil. Notably, Mr. and Mrs. Adachi generously donated the "Tsugumi 311" toy, and Mrs. Adachi, a toy consultant, also provided valuable insights for this book.

Enjoy Coloring with Safe Paint

Unleash your creativity and infuse life into your toy with vibrant hues! There's no need for concern about painting items that will be in regular contact with skin. There are a variety of child-safe, non-toxic paints available in the market. In this section, we'll walk you through the basic method of painting. Armed with a few key tips, you'll be well on your way to achieving a stunning finish. Additionally, we'll explore techniques for painting those small, intricate parts of the toy. So let's dive in.

TOOLS

Paint

When painting wooden toys, non-toxic, child-safe paints are essential. These could be acrylics, water-based paints, or milk paints. Each has its own unique characteristics: acrylics dry quickly and offer vibrant colors; water-based paints are easy to use and clean; milk paints provide an antique, grainy look. Some popular options for nontoxic paints are Crayola® Washable Kids Paint, FolkArt® Acrylic Paint, and Apple Barrel® Acrylic Paint, though there are many others on the market. It's always recommended to check that any paint used is certified nontoxic and safe for children.

Waste Cloth

It is convenient to buy waste cloths at a mass retailer and prepare plenty of them. Alternatively, you can use old cotton materials like T-shirts as a substitute. Having an ample supply is essential for various purposes, including wiping off excess paint, cleaning brushes, and protecting surfaces during painting. By being well-prepared with an abundant quantity of waste cloth, you can ensure a smoother painting process and maintain a clean working environment.

Brushes

The choice of brush can significantly impact the finish of your painted wooden toys. For larger surface areas, a flat brush can provide a smooth, even coat. For finer details, a smaller, round-tipped brush would be more suitable. Synthetic brushes are usually suitable for acrylic and water-based paints, while natural bristle brushes are ideal for oil-based paints.

Sandpaper

Sandpaper is used to prepare the wooden toy surface before painting and between coats of paint. This preparation helps to create a smooth surface for paint application and promotes better adhesion of the paint. It's suggested to start with a coarse-grit sandpaper to remove any rough areas, then move to a medium-grit for general smoothing, and finally use a fine-grit sandpaper for finishing. Always sand along the grain of the wood, not against it.

Brush Cleaning Liquid

Keeping brushes clean is crucial for their longevity and the quality of your paint application. Water is typically sufficient for cleaning brushes used with water-based paints. For oil-based paints, a solvent like mineral spirits or turpentine is necessary. There are also commercial brush cleaners available that can condition the brush bristles, keeping them soft and pliable. Always rinse the brushes thoroughly after cleaning, reshape the bristles, and allow them to dry completely before storage.

How to Paint

Step 1: Sanding
Start by sanding the toy to create a smooth surface. Start with coarse-grit sandpaper to remove any rough areas, and then progress to a medium-grit. Finally, finish with a fine-grit sandpaper for a polished, smooth surface. Always sand along the grain of the wood. After sanding, wipe away the dust with a clean, dry cloth.

Step 2: Mixing the Paint
Before painting, thoroughly mix the paint in the can by stirring it about 30 times. It is recommended to use a mixing stick, such as a craft stick, to ensure the paint is well-blended. This helps to distribute any settled pigments and achieve a consistent color.

Step 3: Preparing the Brush
Dip the tip of the brush into the paint, submerging it approximately one-third of its length. Then, remove any excess paint from the brush by lightly wiping it against the edge of the paint container. This step ensures the right amount of paint is applied and prevents excessive dripping.

Step 4: Painting
Choose a nontoxic, child-safe paint. Use a flat brush for larger surface areas, and a smaller brush for detailed areas. Apply the paint evenly over the surface of the toy. Be sure to allow each coat of paint to dry thoroughly before adding another. This could take a few hours to a full day, depending on the paint and the environmental conditions.

Remember, the key to a great finish is patience—don't rush the drying process between coats of paint, and always take the time to prepare the toy's surface properly before you begin painting. Happy crafting!

STORY OF TREE

Tokyo Toy Museum

The Tokyo Toy Museum is a captivating exhibition space that showcases toys from around the globe as well as works created by Japanese artists. Unlike traditional museums, here you can fully engage with the toys, holding them in your hand and immersing yourself in the joy of play. The museum offers a unique opportunity to interact with toys and experience a natural connection with trees.

At the Tokyo Toy Museum, the focus is not only on the toys themselves but also on the relationship between "trees" and "people." The activities organized by the museum aim to foster an appreciation for nature and promote sustainable practices. Visitors are encouraged to explore the interplay between toys and the environment, gaining a deeper understanding of the significance of trees and their role in shaping our lives.

Through hands-on experiences, educational programs, and exhibitions, the Tokyo Toy Museum creates an inclusive and enriching environment where people of all ages can engage with toys and develop a deeper appreciation for the natural world.

What Is the Tokyo Toy Museum?

The Tokyo Toy Museum is operated by the NPO Japan Good Toy Committee. It is housed in a former elementary school building in Shinjuku Ward, which creates a unique and nostalgic atmosphere that is enjoyable for both children and adults.

When visiting the museum, the toy curators, wearing their distinctive red aprons, warmly welcome visitors. The museum was meticulously prepared for its opening, including the transportation of wood for the interior, turning it into an artful space. As you step inside, a sense of excitement and anticipation fills the air, inviting you to explore and play with the toys on display.

The museum features various themed exhibition rooms, such as the Japanese traditional toy room called "Toy no Machi Aka" and the globally-inspired "Toy Town Yellow." Each room showcases carefully selected toys, and the ingenuity of the displays captures the imagination. You might find yourself getting lost in the enchanting world of wooden balls or enjoying the soft light filtering through the wooden sandbox. One particularly recommended area is the "Baby Kiiku Hiro" room, where you can experience a cozy and inviting space that resembles a tree.

With a dedicated play area and a relaxed atmosphere, the Tokyo Toy Museum is a place where both parents and children can enjoy themselves and engage with the natural world. It's a delightful destination to immerse yourself in the joy of play and connect with the wonders of nature. Why not plan a visit and experience it for yourself? Learn more at https://art-play.or.jp/ttm/.

Corridor inside the hotel. It's a nostalgic feeling, like visiting a school.

A "wooden sandbox" where you can play with about 20,000 wooden balls. Very popular with children.

In the special exhibition room, events that broaden the horizons of toy culture, such as Japanese folk toy exhibitions, are popular.

"Baby Tree Education Plaza" for babies aged 0 to 2 years old. Sit on the cedar floor and play with wooden toys to your heart's content.

The floor of the "Baby tree nursery plaza". The 3cm thick cedar wood keeps you warm, so you can sit comfortably and play for long periods of time. Even if a child drops a toy and it gets dented, if you put a damp cloth on it when you go home, it will be back to normal the next morning.

TOKYO TOY MUSEUM ACTIVITIES

Toy Consultant

The Toy Consultant program is the leading comprehensive toy certification in Japan with a rich 25-year history. It aims to cultivate individuals who possess deep knowledge and expertise in the field of toys. The program focuses on developing professionals who can effectively utilize toys as communication tools, including the ability to select appropriate toys for activities involving the elderly.

Participants who successfully complete the Toy Consultant program are awarded a free toy set, which serves as a valuable resource for their work. Currently, there are around 214 locations nationwide where events, such as toy concerts, are held on an almost daily basis. These events provide opportunities for individuals to showcase their expertise and share their knowledge with others in their respective regions.

The Toy Consultant program plays a crucial role in fostering a greater understanding and appreciation of the significance of toys in various contexts. It serves as a platform for the exchange of ideas and best practices, contributing to the continuous improvement and innovation of the toy industry in Japan.

Promoting Wood Education

The Forestry Agency in Japan is currently promoting "wood education" to address the declining awareness and appreciation of trees. Despite being the world's third-largest forest-holding country with 70% of its land area covered by forests, the significance of trees seems to be diminishing in recent times. In the past, wood was a versatile material that could be shaped and repaired, allowing people to develop a deep connection with it. However, with the advent of new materials like plastic, the unique properties and unpredictability of wood have been somewhat overlooked.

The aim of "wood education" extends beyond familiarizing individuals with trees. It also involves passing down traditional techniques and life wisdom that have been handed down through generations. Teaching children proper woodworking skills, for instance, not only imparts practical knowledge but also instills a zest for life and an appreciation for craftsmanship. By embracing "wood education," Japan seeks to rekindle the relationship between people and trees, preserving and sharing the valuable knowledge and skills associated with wood.

Wood education serves as a means to cultivate a deeper understanding of nature's resources and the sustainable utilization of wood. By nurturing a generation that appreciates the beauty and functionality of wood, Japan aims to ensure the continued preservation and wise management of its forests for future generations.

Wood Start Declaration

In Japan, despite the historical dominance of wooden toy production in Europe, there is still a strong preference for wooden toys among children. The desire to play with toys made from local wood stems from Japan's abundant forest resources and the presence of skilled craftsmen with exceptional woodworking techniques. This very notion led to the establishment of the Tokyo Toy Museum, with the belief that toys made from local wood can offer unique and enriching play experiences.

The "Do Start Declaration" initiative has been spreading to municipalities across the country. As part of this effort, newborns are presented with toys made from local wood, which not only contribute to the safe and enjoyable play experiences of children but also foster the revitalization of local communities. Toy artists supervise the creation of attractive and safe toys that support parenting and child-rearing activities. While many parenting support activities tend to be led by women, the approach of spreading the goodness of wood education has been successful in engaging a wider range of participants, including older men and students who may not have previously had much exposure to it.

The natural charm of wooden toys appeals to people of all ages, and the Tokyo Toy Museum serves as a space where individuals can explore their interests beyond just raising children. It has become a place where the enjoyment and benefits of wooden toys can be shared and experienced by everyone.

The selection of "Good Toys" showcases excellent toys available in the Japanese market, with the aim of introducing them to a wider audience. These toys not only facilitate immediate connections and interactions between people but also include original works developed through discussions with toy makers to enhance the enjoyment of play.

"Mokuiku Caravan"

The Tokyo Toy Museum is actively engaging with rural areas through the "Moving Toy Museum" initiative. This event involves bringing the museum's toys to rural locations, connecting with local volunteers, university students, and wood craftsmen. The goal is to establish bonds with the local community by providing opportunities to engage with wooden toys.

By collaborating with local volunteers, university students, and wood craftsmen, the "Moving Toy Museum" creates a platform for sharing the joy of wooden toys and fostering connections within the community. This initiative not only brings the magic of the Tokyo Toy Museum to rural areas but also supports local economies and promotes the value of wooden toy craftsmanship. It is a wonderful way to bridge the gap between urban and rural communities and create lasting connections through the universal language of play.

"Good Toy" is a prestigious recognition given to exceptional toys available in Japan, and we aim to bring these toys to a wider audience. Toys have the remarkable ability to foster immediate communication and connection, even among strangers.

We also have original creations developed in collaboration with toy makers to ensure our customers have an enjoyable play experience.

"Child-rearing Salon's Tree Education Class"

The "Baby Tree Nursery Plaza" is a unique initiative taking place in various companies and local government buildings, offering nursery and store spaces dedicated to wood materials. These spaces provide a sanctuary of calm, warmth, and healing in our fast-paced society, allowing people of all ages to interact with wood and experience its soothing qualities.

Through playing with wooden toys, exploring wooden structures, or simply enjoying the natural beauty of wood, individuals can find respite and a deeper connection to nature. The "Baby Tree Nursery Plaza" promotes the value of wood materials and fosters appreciation for their ability to bring comfort and serenity to our lives.

Courtesy: Certified NPO Japan
Good Toy Committee Baby Tree
Education Department

Kyouko Ishii

Patterns

P. 90 RAINBOW PUZZLE

DRAWING A: HOLE LAYOUT

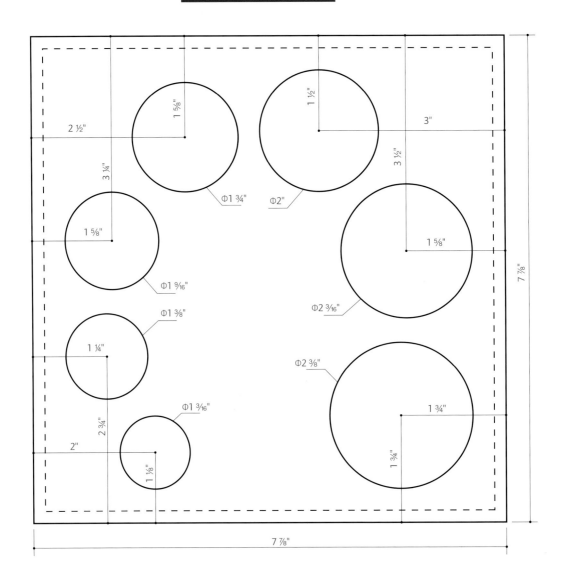

DRAWING B: MAIN BODY AND BACK BOARD

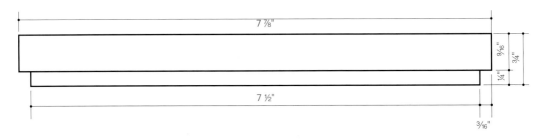

DOG PULL TOY

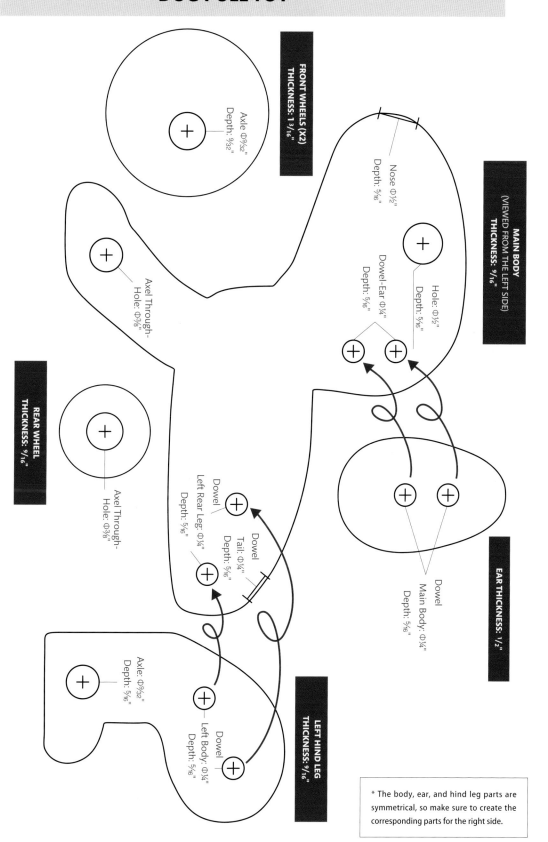

FRONT WHEELS (X2)
THICKNESS: 1 3/16"

Axle Φ9/32"
Depth: 9/32"

MAIN BODY
(VIEWED FROM THE LEFT SIDE)
THICKNESS: 9/16"

Nose Φ1/2"
Depth: 5/16"

Dowel-Ear Φ1/4"
Depth: 5/16"

Hole: Φ1/2"
Depth: 5/16"

Axel Through-
Hole: Φ3/8"

REAR WHEEL
THICKNESS: 9/16"

Axel Through-
Hole: Φ3/8"

Dowel
Left Rear Leg: Φ1/4"
Depth: 5/16"

Dowel
Tail: Φ1/4"
Depth: 5/16"

EAR THICKNESS: 1/2"

Dowel
Main Body: Φ1/4"
Depth: 5/16"

Axle: Φ9/32"
Depth: 5/16"

Dowel
Left Body: Φ1/4"
Depth: 5/16"

LEFT HIND LEG
THICKNESS: 9/16"

* The body, ear, and hind leg parts are
symmetrical, so make sure to create the
corresponding parts for the right side.

PAPER PATTERN FOR STAR PARTS (ACTUAL SIZE)

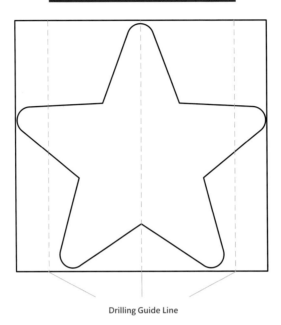

Drilling Guide Line

UFO PARTS PAPER PATTERN (ACTUAL SIZE)

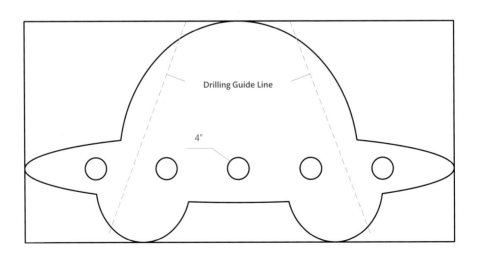

Drilling Guide Line

4"

"R" indicates the radius of the curve (e.g. R3⁄16" = curve with 3⁄16" [5mm] radius).
"Φ" indicates the diameter of the circle or hole (Φ5⁄16" is a 5⁄16" [8mm] diameter circle).

DRAWING A

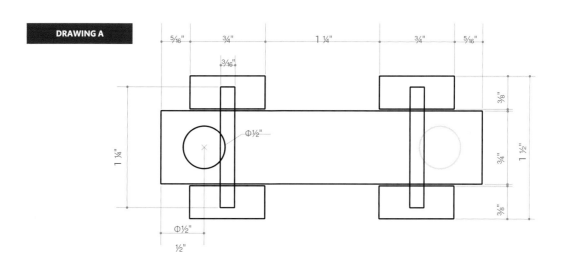

DRAWING B

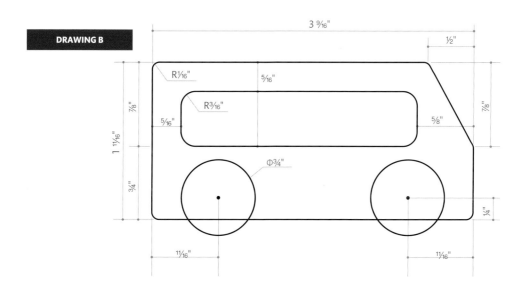

DRAWING C

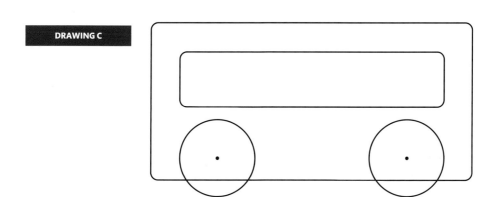

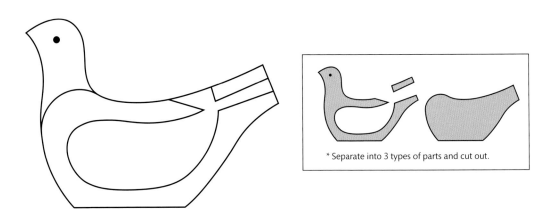

P. 42   **BIRD WHISTLE**

* Separate into 3 types of parts and cut out.

P. 46   **PUZZLE CUBE**

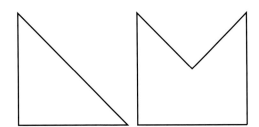

**DRAWING A:
COLOR PAPER
PATTERN**

**DRAWING B:
COLOR DEVELOPMENT DIAGRAM**

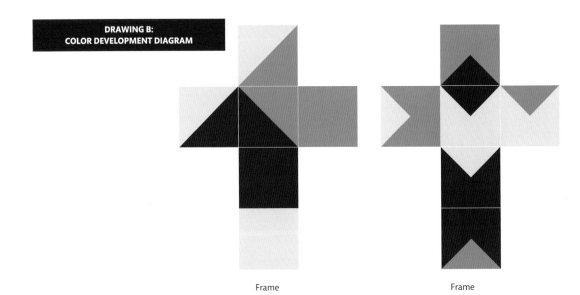

Frame   Frame

"R" indicates the radius of the curve (e.g. R³⁄₁₆" = curve with ³⁄₁₆" [5mm] radius).
"Φ" indicates the diameter of the circle or hole (Φ⁵⁄₁₆" is a ⁵⁄₁₆" [8mm] diameter circle).

156

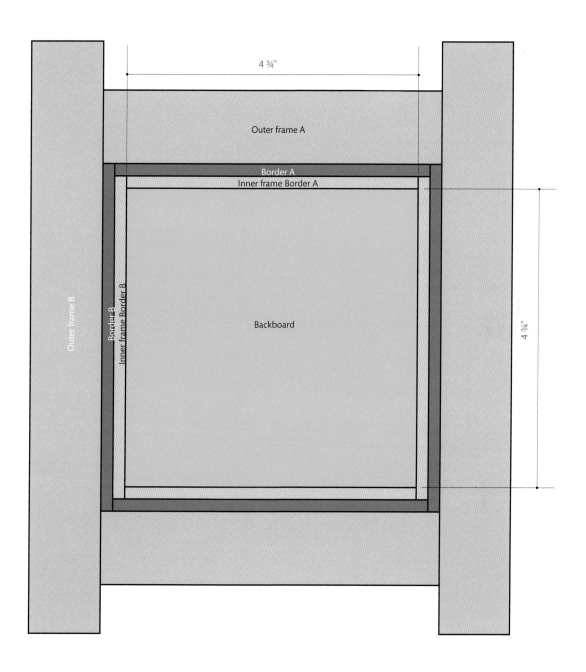

4 ¾"

Outer frame A

Border A

Inner frame Border A

Outer frame B

Border B

Inner frame Border B

Backboard

4 ¾"

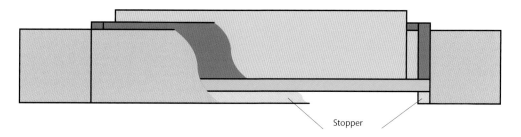

Stopper

A: SIDE DIMENSIONS
(HEAD/TORSO/TAIL)

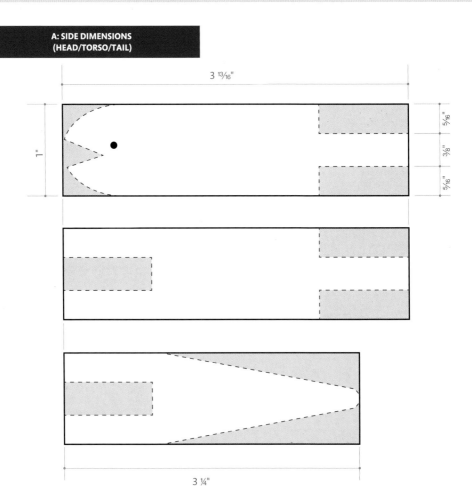

3 ¹³⁄₁₆"

1"

⁵⁄₁₆"

³⁄₈"

⁵⁄₁₆"

3 ¼"

DRAWING B:
TOP AND BOTTOM STENCIL

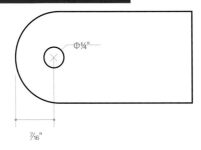

Φ¼"

⁷⁄₁₆"

"R" indicates the radius of the curve (e.g. R³⁄₁₆" = curve with ³⁄₁₆" [5mm] radius).
"Φ" indicates the diameter of the circle or hole (Φ⁵⁄₁₆" is a ⁵⁄₁₆" [8mm] diameter circle).

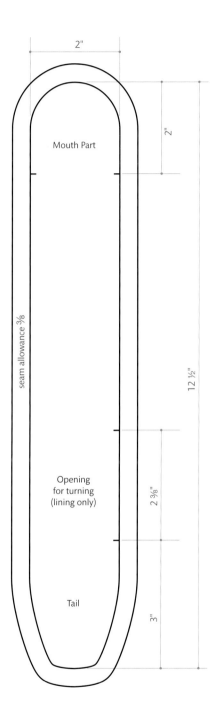

2"

2"

Mouth Part

seam allowance ⅜

12 ½"

Opening
for turning
(lining only)

2 ⅜"

Tail

3"

Note: Since it is reduced to 50%, please enlarge it to 200% when copying and using .

ANIMAL PARTS PATTERN (ACTUAL SIZE)

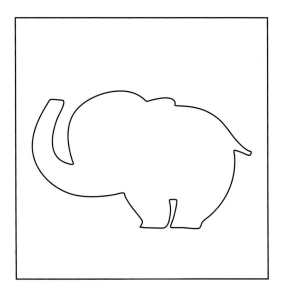

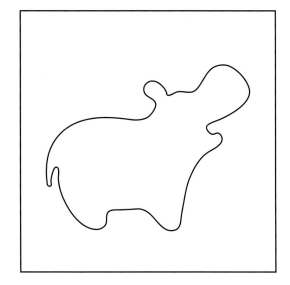

"R" indicates the radius of the curve (e.g. R³⁄₁₆" = curve with ³⁄₁₆" [5mm] radius).
"Φ" indicates the diameter of the circle or hole (Φ⁵⁄₁₆" is a ⁵⁄₁₆" [8mm] diameter circle).

ANIMAL PARTS PATTERN (ACTUAL SIZE)

ROTATING BLANK PATTERN (ACTUAL SIZE)

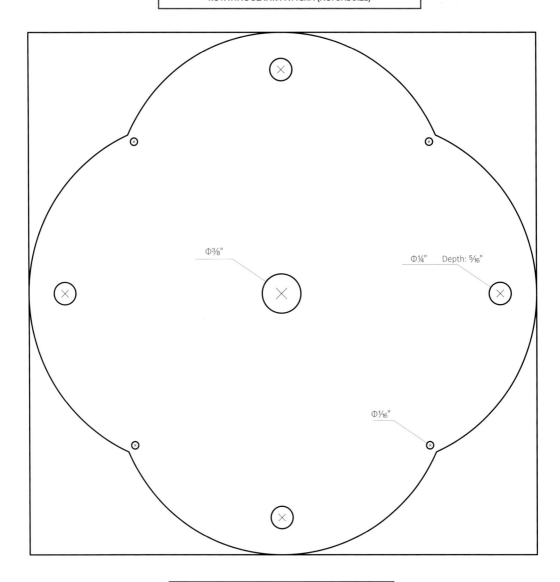

Φ⅜"

Φ¼"   Depth: ⁵⁄₁₆"

Φ¹⁄₁₆"

ANIMAL PARTS PATTERN (ACTUAL SIZE)

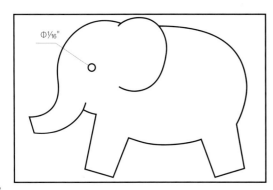

Φ¹⁄₁₆"

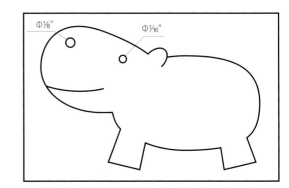

Φ⅛"   Φ¹⁄₁₆"

"R" indicates the radius of the curve (e.g. R³⁄₁₆" = curve with ³⁄₁₆" [5mm] radius).
"Φ" indicates the diameter of the circle or hole (Φ⁵⁄₁₆" is a ⁵⁄₁₆" [8mm] diameter circle).

PEDESTAL PATTERN
(ACTUAL SIZE)

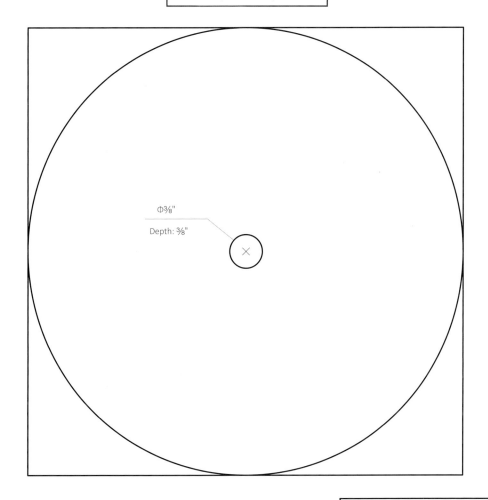

Φ³⁄₈"

Depth: ³⁄₈"

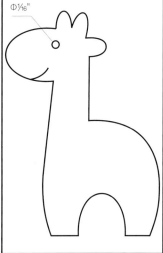

Φ¹⁄₁₆"

ANIMAL PARTS PATTERN (ACTUAL SIZE)

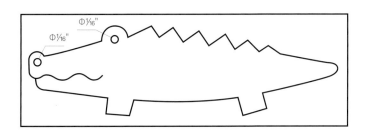

Φ¹⁄₁₆"

Φ¹⁄₁₆"

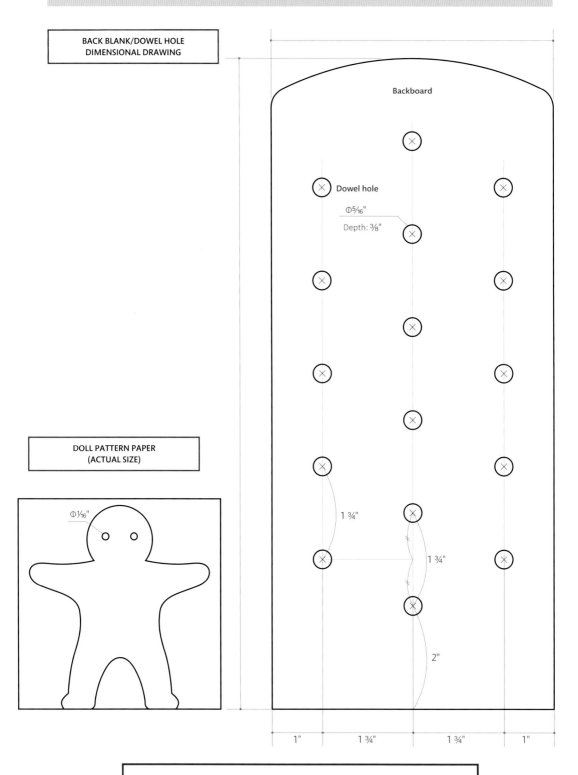

BACK BLANK/DOWEL HOLE
DIMENSIONAL DRAWING

Backboard

Dowel hole

Φ⁵⁄₁₆"
Depth: ³⁄₈"

DOLL PATTERN PAPER
(ACTUAL SIZE)

Φ¹⁄₁₆"

1 ³⁄₄"

1 ³⁄₄"

2"

1"   1 ³⁄₄"   1 ³⁄₄"   1"

"R" indicates the radius of the curve (e.g. R³⁄₁₆" = curve with ³⁄₁₆" [5mm] radius).
"Φ" indicates the diameter of the circle or hole (Φ⁵⁄₁₆" is a ⁵⁄₁₆" [8mm] diameter circle).

TOY HOUSE

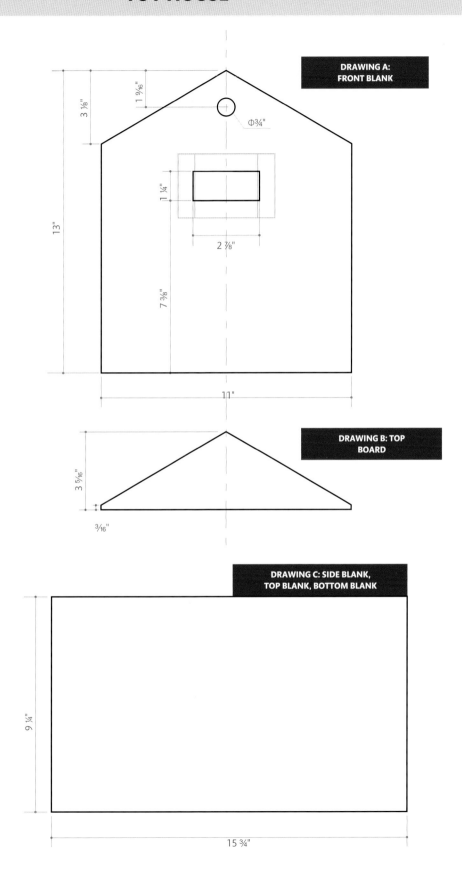

DRAWING A: FRONT BLANK

3 ⅛"

1 ⁹⁄₁₆"

Φ¾"

1 ¼"

2 ⅞"

13"

7 ⅜"

11"

DRAWING B: TOP BOARD

3 ⁵⁄₁₆"

³⁄₁₆"

DRAWING C: SIDE BLANK, TOP BLANK, BOTTOM BLANK

9 ¼"

15 ¾"

DRAWING D:
ASSEMBLY DRAWING (TOP)

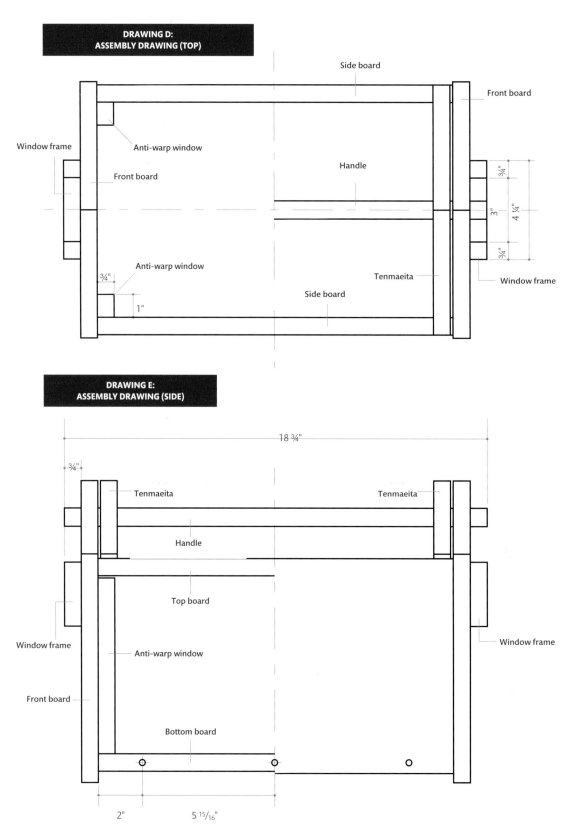

Side board

Front board

Window frame

Anti-warp window

Front board

Handle

¾"

3" 4 ¼"

¾"

Window frame

Anti-warp window

Tenmaeita

¾"

1"

Side board

DRAWING E:
ASSEMBLY DRAWING (SIDE)

18 ¾"

¾"

Tenmaeita

Tenmaeita

Handle

Top board

Window frame

Window frame

Anti-warp window

Front board

Bottom board

2"

5 ¹⁵/₁₆"

"R" indicates the radius of the curve (e.g. R³⁄₁₆" = curve with ³⁄₁₆" [5mm] radius).
"Φ" indicates the diameter of the circle or hole (Φ⁵⁄₁₆" is a ⁵⁄₁₆" [8mm] diameter circle).

**DRAWING F:
ASSEMBLY DRAWING
(FRONT)**

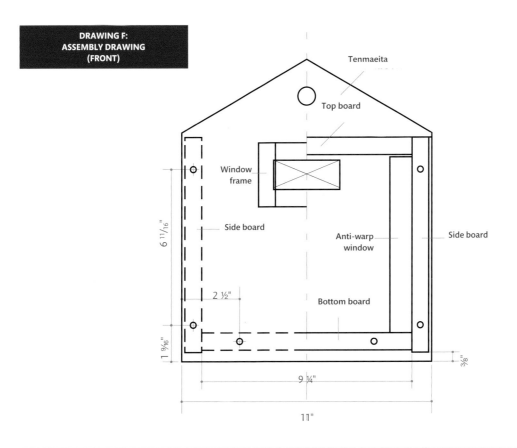

Tenmaeita

Top board

Window frame

Side board

Anti-warp window

Side board

Bottom board

6 ¹¹⁄₁₆"

2 ½"

1 ⁹⁄₁₆"

³⁄₈"

9 ¼"

11"

P. 112 **SWIMMING FISH**

**FISH PATTERN PAPER
(ACTUAL SIZE)**

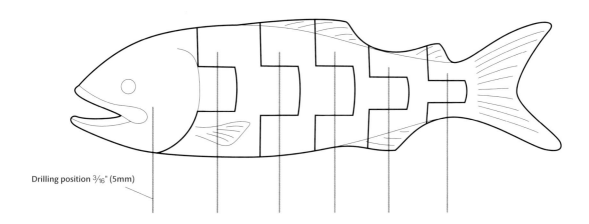

Drilling position ³⁄₁₆" (5mm)

* Since it is reduced to 50%, please enlarge it to 200% when copying and using.

* The black circle is ³⁄₈" (10mm), and the blue circle is ⁷⁄₁₆" (11mm).

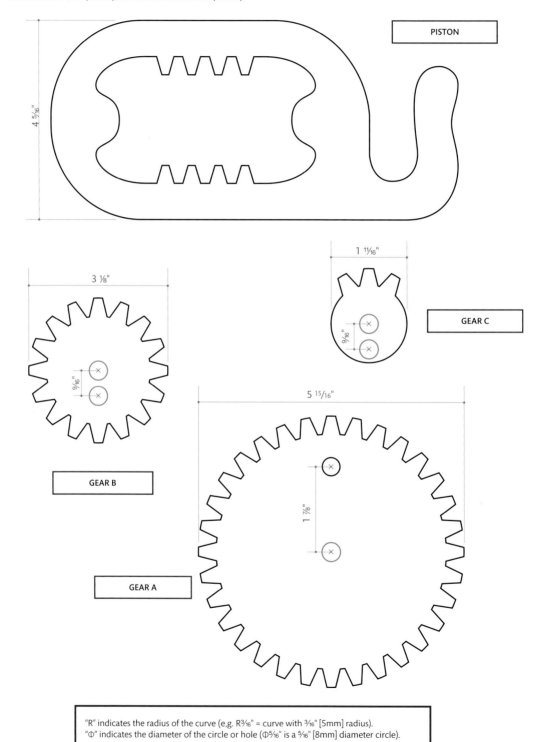

PISTON

4 ⁵⁄₁₆"

1 ¹¹⁄₁₆"

GEAR C

⁹⁄₁₆"

3 ⅛"

⁹⁄₁₆"

GEAR B

5 ¹⁵⁄₁₆"

1 ⅞"

GEAR A

"R" indicates the radius of the curve (e.g. R³⁄₁₆" = curve with ³⁄₁₆" [5mm] radius).
"Φ" indicates the diameter of the circle or hole (Φ⁵⁄₁₆" is a ⁵⁄₁₆" [8mm] diameter circle).

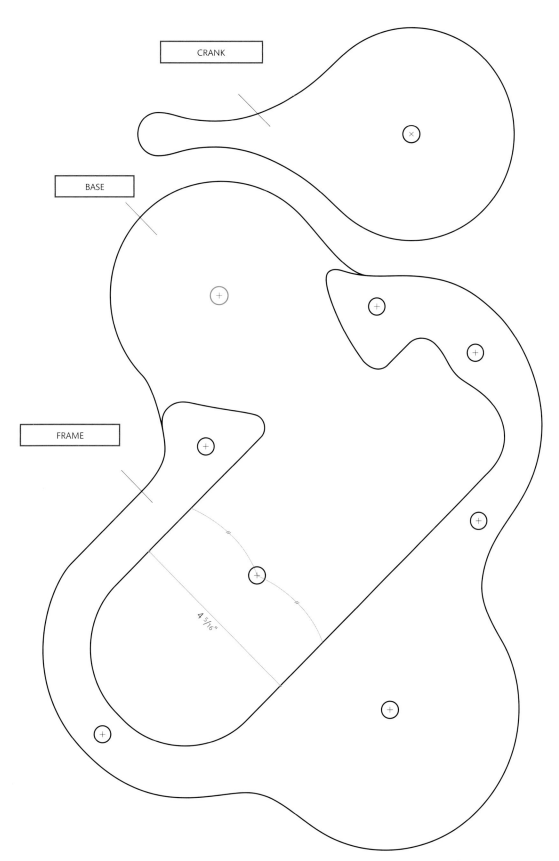

CRANK

BASE

FRAME

4 5/16"

Since the frame and base are overlapped, please make two copies.

ROBOT WALKER WAGON

DRAWING A: DRAWING OF EACH PART

Cargo bed side board x 2 stud material

4 ⅛"

3 ¾"

3 ¾"

1 ³⁄₁₆"

4 "

5 ¹⁵⁄₁₆"

⅜"

1 ³⁄₁₆"

Φ⁵⁄₁₆"   1 "

Φ¾"

1 "

⁹⁄₁₆"

2 ⅜"

¾"

Φ⁵⁄₁₆"

1 ¹¹⁄₁₆"

1 "

Φ⁵⁄₁₆"

1 ³⁄₁₆"

1 "

Φ⁵⁄₁₆"

3 "

Φ¾"

5 ¾"

R2"

¾"

2 "

Handle arm (x2) 1x2 material

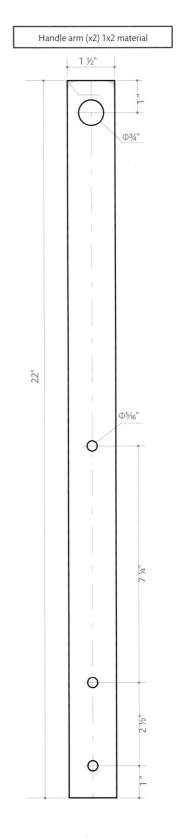

1 ½"

1 "

Φ¾"

22"

Φ⁵⁄₁₆"

7 ¼"

2 ½"

1 "

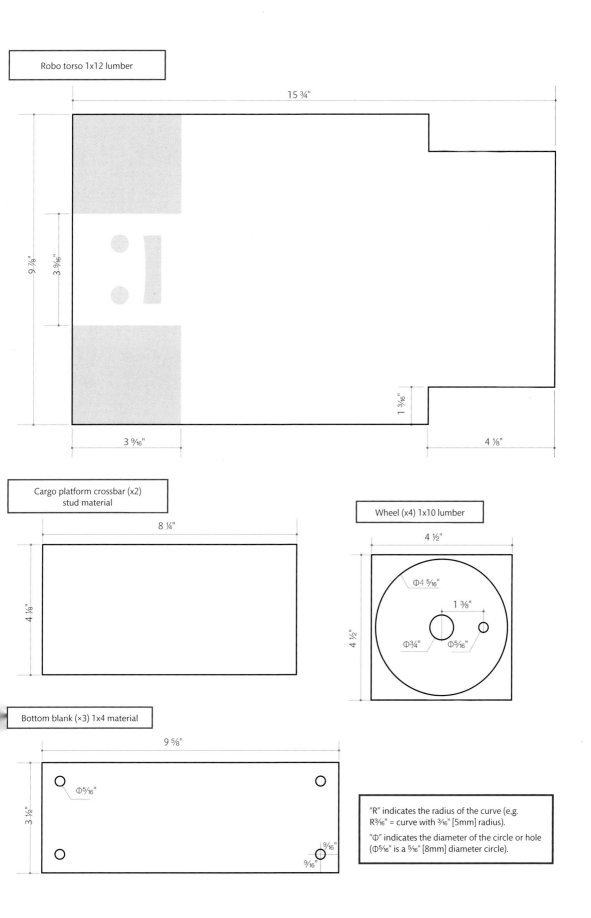

Robo torso 1x12 lumber

15 ¾"

9 ⅞"

3 ⁹⁄₁₆"

3 ⁹⁄₁₆"

1 ³⁄₁₆"

4 ⅛"

Cargo platform crossbar (x2)
stud material

8 ¼"

4 ⅛"

Wheel (x4) 1x10 lumber

4 ½"

Φ4 ⁵⁄₁₆"

1 ⅜"

Φ¾"

Φ⁵⁄₁₆"

4 ½"

Bottom blank (×3) 1x4 material

9 ⅝"

3 ½"

Φ⁵⁄₁₆"

⁹⁄₁₆"

⁹⁄₁₆"

"R" indicates the radius of the curve (e,g,
R³⁄₁₆" = curve with ³⁄₁₆" [5mm] radius).

"Φ" indicates the diameter of the circle or hole
(Φ⁵⁄₁₆" is a ⁵⁄₁₆" [8mm] diameter circle).

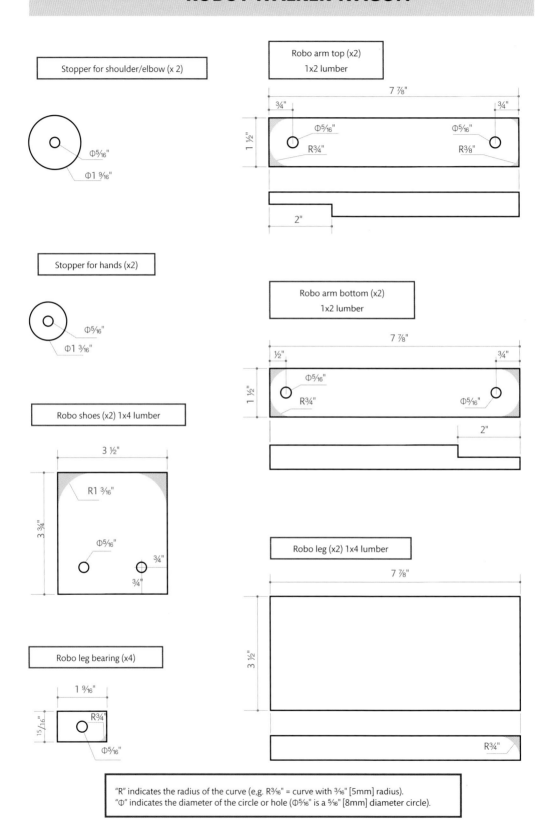

Stopper for shoulder/elbow (x 2)

Φ5/16"
Φ1 9/16"

Robo arm top (x2)
1x2 lumber

7 7/8"
3/4"
3/4"
1 1/2"
Φ5/16"
Φ5/16"
R3/4"
R3/8"
2"

Stopper for hands (x2)

Φ5/16"
Φ1 3/16"

Robo arm bottom (x2)
1x2 lumber

7 7/8"
1/2"
3/4"
1 1/2"
Φ5/16"
Φ5/16"
R3/4"
Φ5/16"
2"

Robo shoes (x2) 1x4 lumber

3 1/2"
R1 3/16"
3 3/4"
Φ5/16"
3/4"
3/4"

Robo leg (x2) 1x4 lumber

7 7/8"
3 1/2"
R3/4"

Robo leg bearing (x4)

1 9/16"
15/16"
R3/4"
Φ5/16"

"R" indicates the radius of the curve (e.g. R3/16" = curve with 3/16" [5mm] radius).
"Φ" indicates the diameter of the circle or hole (Φ5/16" is a 5/16" [8mm] diameter circle).

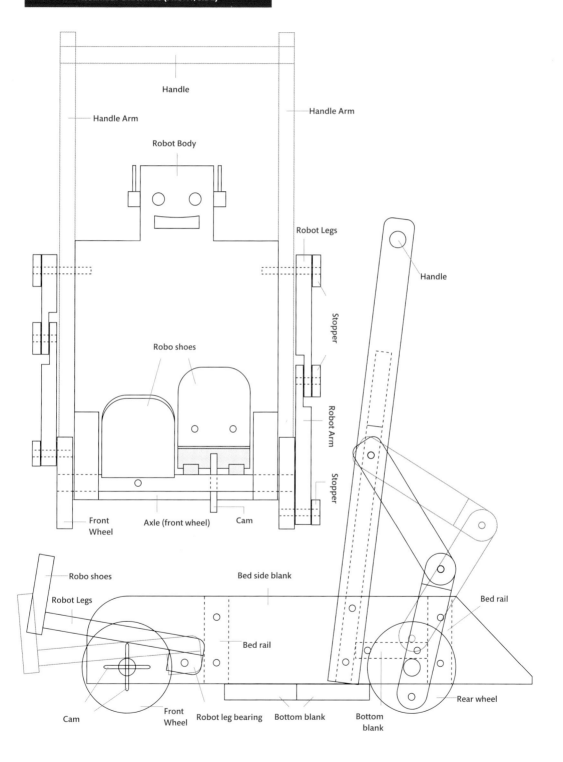

Handle

Handle Arm

Handle Arm

Robot Body

Handle

Robot Legs

Stopper

Robo shoes

Robot Arm

Stopper

Front
Wheel

Axle (front wheel)

Cam

Robo shoes

Bed side blank

Bed rail

Robot Legs

Bed rail

Cam

Front
Wheel

Robot leg bearing

Bottom blank

Bottom
blank

Rear wheel

DRAWING B:
ASSEMBLY DRAWING (BOTTOM)

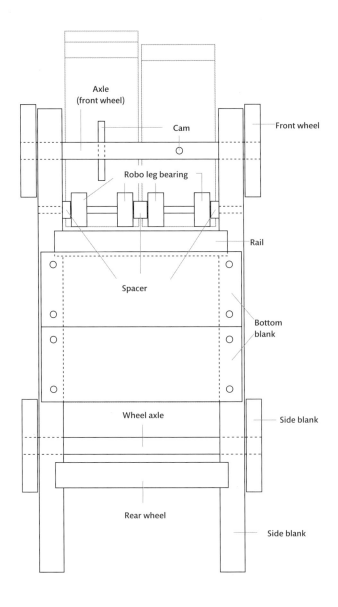

Axle
(front wheel)

Cam

Front wheel

Robo leg bearing

Rail

Spacer

Bottom
blank

Wheel axle

Side blank

Rear wheel

Side blank

"R" indicates the radius of the curve (e.g. R³⁄₁₆" = curve with ³⁄₁₆" [5mm] radius).
"Φ" indicates the diameter of the circle or hole (Φ⁵⁄₁₆" is a ⁵⁄₁₆" [8mm] diameter circle).

DRAWING A:
DIMENSIONS OF EACH PART

*Only shaped parts are listed

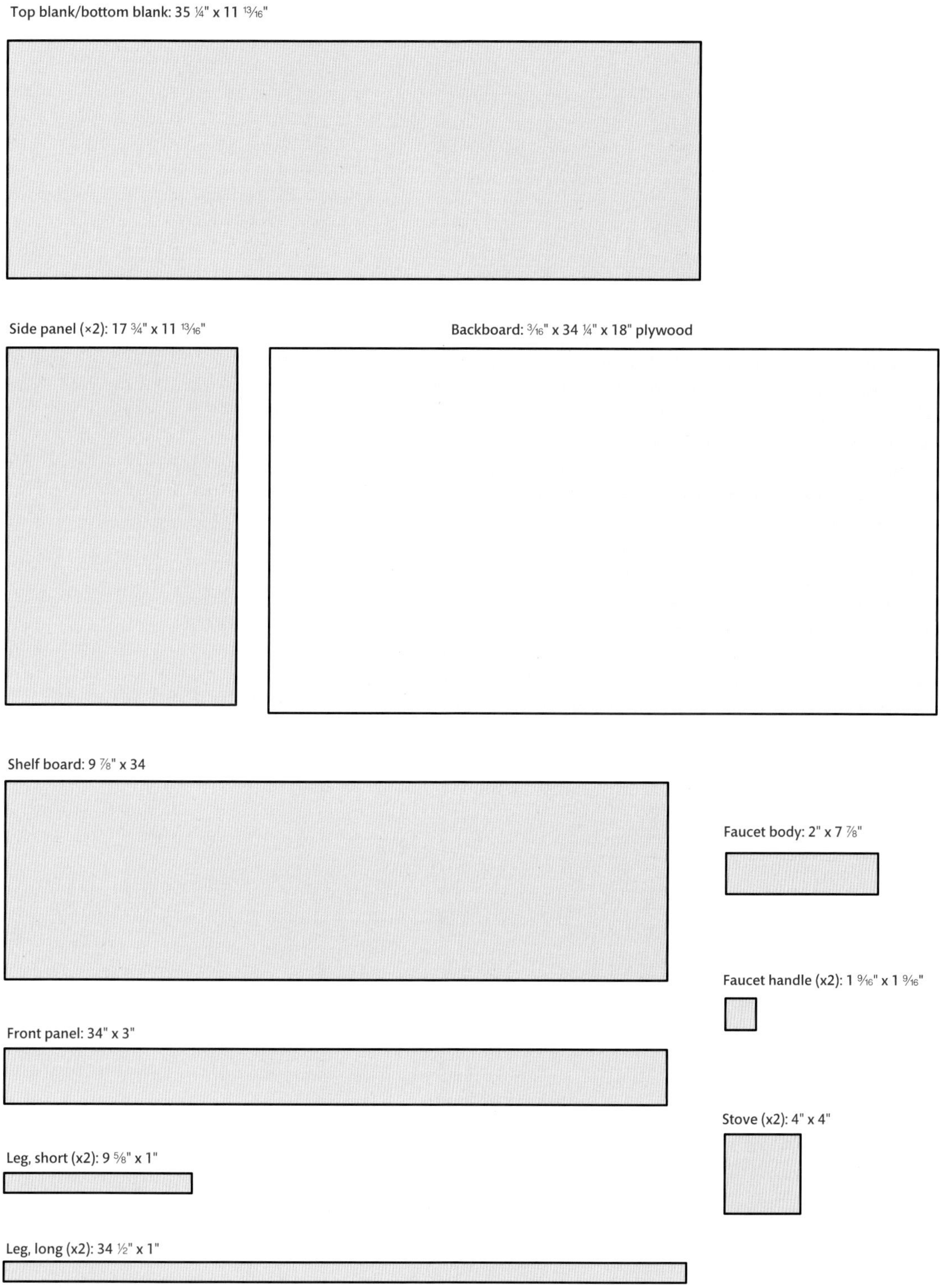

Top blank/bottom blank: 35 ¼" x 11 ¹³⁄₁₆"

Side panel (×2): 17 ¾" x 11 ¹³⁄₁₆"

Backboard: ³⁄₁₆" x 34 ¼" x 18" plywood

Shelf board: 9 ⅞" x 34

Faucet body: 2" x 7 ⅞"

Faucet handle (x2): 1 ⁹⁄₁₆" x 1 ⁹⁄₁₆"

Front panel: 34" x 3"

Leg, short (x2): 9 ⅝" x 1"

Stove (x2): 4" x 4"

Leg, long (x2): 34 ½" x 1"

DRAWING B:
ASSEMBLY DRAWING

TOP
SURFACE

BOTTOM
SURFACE

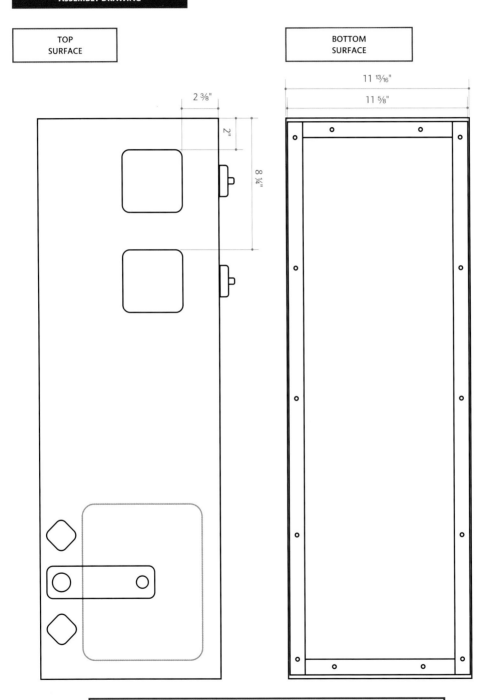

"R" indicates the radius of the curve (e.g. R³⁄₁₆" = curve with ³⁄₁₆" [5mm] radius).
"Φ" indicates the diameter of the circle or hole (Φ⁵⁄₁₆" is a ⁵⁄₁₆" [8mm] diameter circle).

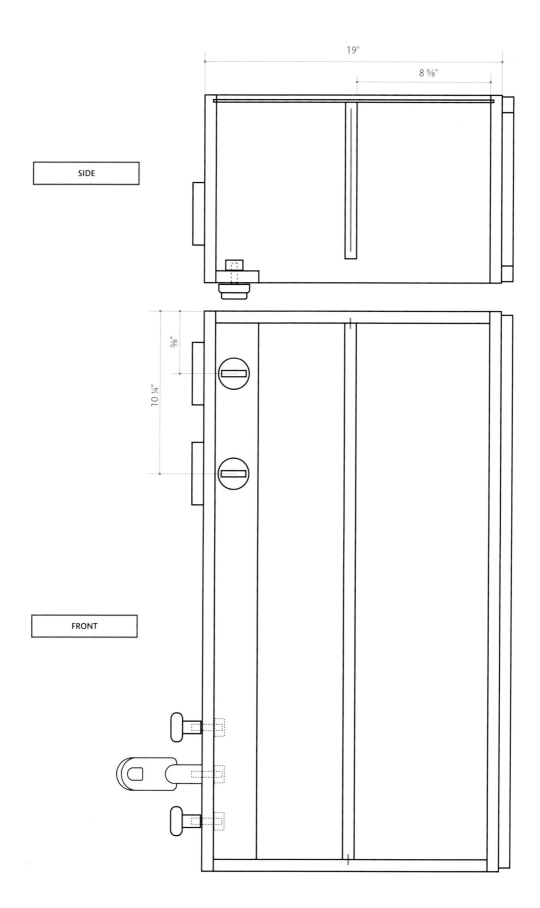

SIDE

FRONT

19"

8 ⅝"

3⁄8"

10 ¼"

A: DRAWING OF EACH PART

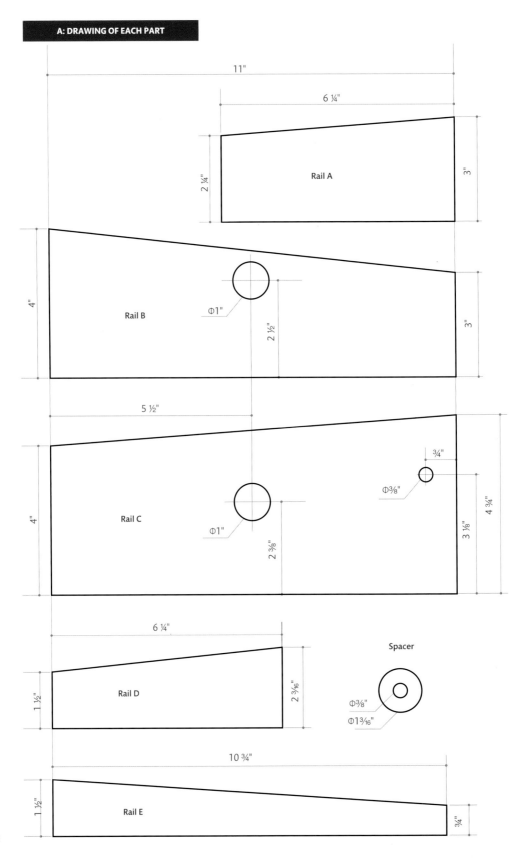

"R" indicates the radius of the curve (e.g. R³⁄₁₆" = curve with ³⁄₁₆" [5mm] radius).
"Φ" indicates the diameter of the circle or hole (Φ⁵⁄₁₆" is a ⁵⁄₁₆" [8mm] diameter circle).

Roulette

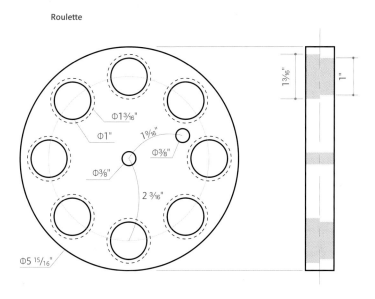

Foundation

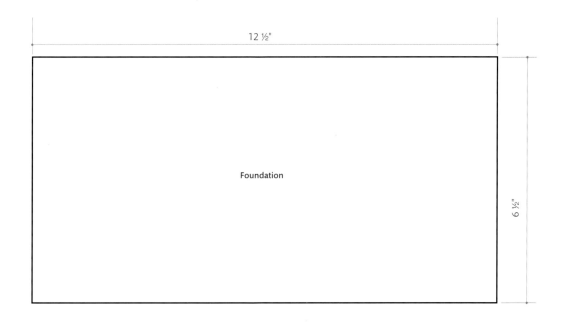

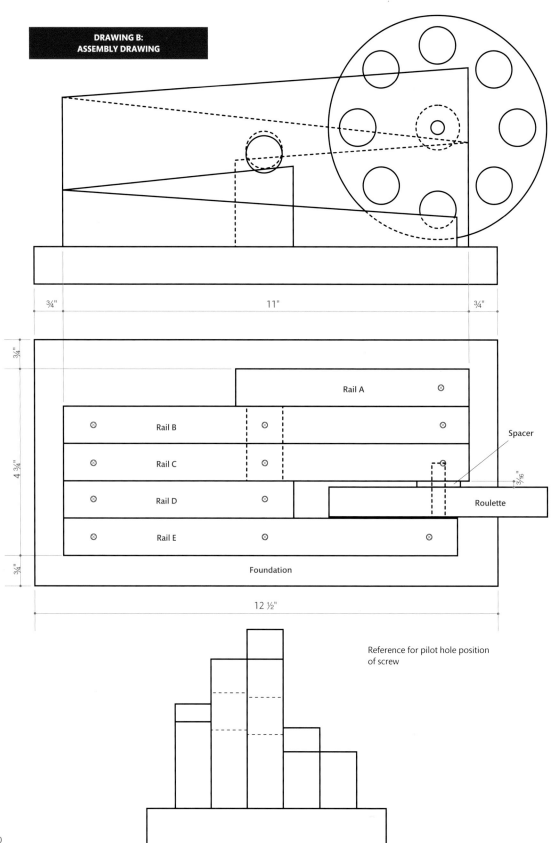

**DRAWING B:
ASSEMBLY DRAWING**

¾"   11"   ¾"

¾"

Rail A   ⊗

Rail B   ⊗

Rail C   ⊗

Spacer

Roulette

3/16"

Rail D   ⊗

Rail E   ⊗

Foundation

4 ¾"

¾"

12 ½"

Reference for pilot hole position
of screw

"R" indicates the radius of the curve (e.g. R³⁄₁₆" = curve with ³⁄₁₆" [5mm] radius).
"Φ" indicates the diameter of the circle or hole (Φ⁵⁄₁₆" is a ⁵⁄₁₆" [8mm] diameter circle).

DRAWING C:
RAIL DRAWING

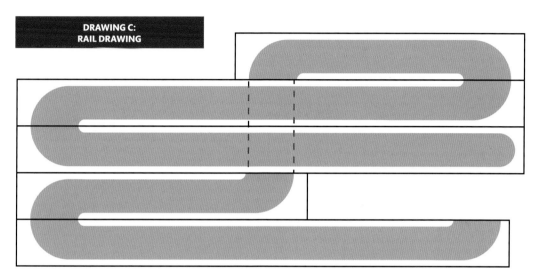

DRAWING D:
RAIL CURVE PATTERN (ACTUAL SIZE)

DRAWING E:
RAIL GROOVE CROSS SECTION

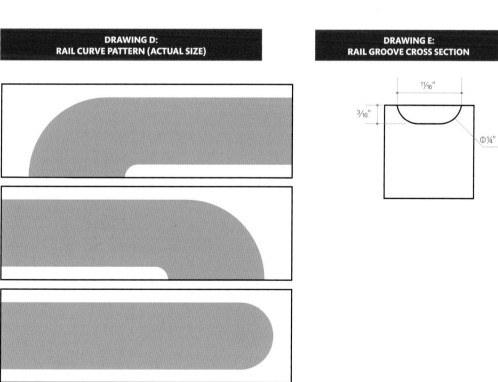

Conversion Table

Please note that metric conversions are not exact equivalents of US sizes. Instead, they reflect the closest common metric measurement when rounded.

US	Metric	US	Metric	US	Metric
1/16"	2mm	2 1/4"	58mm	7 3/8"	188mm
1/8"	3mm	2 3/8"	60mm	7 1/2"	190mm
3/16"	5mm	2 1/2"	65mm	7 7/8"	200mm
1/4"	6mm	2 3/4"	70mm	8 1/4"	210mm
5/16"	8mm	2 7/8"	73mm	8 5/8"	220mm
3/8"	10mm	3"	76mm	9 1/4"	235mm
7/16"	11mm	3 1/8"	80mm	9 5/8"	245mm
1/2"	12–13mm	3 3/16"	81mm	9 7/8"	250mm
9/16"	14–15mm	3 1/4"	83–84mm	10 1/4"	260mm
5/8"	16mm	3 5/16"	85mm	10 3/4"	270mm
11/16"	18mm	3 1/2"	89mm	11"	280mm
3/4"	20mm	3 9/16"	90mm	11 3/16"	285mm
7/8"	23mm	3 3/4"	95mm	11 5/8"	295mm
1"	25mm	4"	100mm	12 1/2"	320mm
1 1/8"	29mm	4 1/8"	105mm	13"	330mm
1 3/16"	30mm	4 1/4"	108mm	15 3/4"	400mm
1 1/4"	32–33mm	4 5/16"	110–111mm	17 3/4"	450mm
1 3/8"	35mm	4 1/2"	115mm	18"	460mm
1 1/2"	38–39mm	4 3/4"	120mm	18 3/4"	476mm
1 9/16"	40mm	5 1/2"	140mm	19"	485mm
1 5/8"	41mm	5 3/4"	145mm	22"	560mm
1 11/16"	43mm	5 15/16"	150mm	34"	865mm
1 3/4"	45mm	6 1/4"	160mm	34 1/4"	870mm
1 7/8"	47mm	6 1/2"	165mm	35 1/4"	895mm
2"	50mm	6 11/16"	170mm		
2 3/16"	55mm	7 1/4"	185mm		

Index

Note: Page numbers in *italics* indicate projects and patterns (*in parentheses*).